Juan de la Cueva

By RICHARD F. GLENN

Northwestern University

Twayne Publishers, Inc. · New York

ISBN 0-8057-2258-0

MANUFACTURED IN THE UNITED STATES OF AMERICA

This book is affectionately dedicated to
my parents

Preface

The significance of Juan de la Cueva is practically unknown to the English-speaking public. The details of his life have never been recorded in English, and there is no study in this language of his complete works. By means of this volume, I hope to acquaint this large segment of the reading public with a man whose works are invested with the best of post-Renaissance Spain. Convinced that both the social and cultural milieu are inextricably bound to his literary activity, I have attempted to provide a basic introduction to Cueva's contemporaries who constitute the School of Seville. In view of the inaccessibility of all but a very few of Cueva's works, it has not seemed amiss to provide complete summaries of all the major works. Critical and analytical observations follow each, and every genre cultivated by the author is touched upon.

The chronology which is followed in this volume is essentially the same one proposed by Fredrik A. Wulff in 1887, but subsequent contributions to the Cueva biography have been incorporated. Additional dates which bear significantly on the author's epoch are included. The general discussions of Cueva's works depend heavily on the studies of the following authorities who have contributed so much to an understanding of the writer: Wulff, Emmanuel Walberg, Francisco A. de Icaza, Edwin S. Morby, and Anthony Irvine Watson.

Since Cueva's literary significance has been sought almost exclusively in the realm of drama—the plays being the most accessible of all his works—I have devoted a perhaps disproportionate number of chapters to the fourteen extant plays. The classification is based on content rather than the chronological order of performance. Since they were all staged within the short span of three years, nothing is gained by a chronological grouping. Because of the prevailing misconceptions concerning the drama in Seville—and the relative successes or failures of tragedy in particular—it seemed advisable to include an introductory chapter in which to silhouette Cueva's contributions to the drama against the greater historical background.

All quotations are translated for the convenience of the reader. Since none of Cueva's works is available in English, these translations, as well as quotations from other foreign authors, are my own. In the interest of accuracy, I have made no attempt to render Spanish verse as poetry in English. Whenever Spanish is quoted, I have modernized the spelling.

Several criteria governed the limits of the Bibliography. In view of the rarity of Cueva's works and the general unfamiliarity with them, the published works are listed completely. The contents of the manuscripts—found in the Biblioteca Nacional in Madrid and the Biblioteca Colombina in Seville—are referred to frequently in the text and in the notes. References to secondary sources are as complete as possible. Books and articles devoted to Cueva are grouped together. It is hoped that the specialist will find here all significant items pertinent to Cueva. As a result of this coverage, only a very limited selection of useful related background materials could be included.

RICHARD F. GLENN

Evanston, Illinois

Acknowledgments

Special acknowledgment is made to the College of Arts and Sciences of Northwestern University which generously granted a leave of absence in order that this book might be completed. The appreciation of the author is likewise expressed to Professor Francis G. Very who read the book in typescript and whose cogent criticism was of the greatest value in preparation of the final product. Gratitude is also expressed to William S. Cudlipp, III who consented to give of his time to type the manuscript.

Contents

Chronology

1550 Juan de la Cueva de Garoza born about this date in Seville.

1554 Marriage of Crown Prince Philip II to Mary Tudor, Queen of England.

1555 The Spanish Humanist Hernán Núñez published his *Refranes o proverbios en romance* (*Sayings or Proverbs in the Vernacular*).

1556 Abdication of Emperor Charles I in favor of Philip II.

1563 The Council of Trent closed, and construction of the Escorial began.

1567 Juan de la Cueva's infatuation with Felipa de la Paz began. His first attempts at amatory verse in the Petrarchan vein date from this period.

1568 Juan de Mal Lara published his *Filosofía vulgar* (*Folk Philosophy*).

1570 Mal Lara published his description of the festivities in honor of Philip II's entrance into Seville.

1571 Naval victory of the Christian flotilla over the Ottoman forces at Lepanto. Death of Mal Lara and the occupation of his chair at the School for Humanities and Grammar by Diego Girón.

1574 Juan de la Cueva sailed for Mexico with his younger brother Claudio. Lope de Rueda's troupe of players performed in the open air in Seville from about this date.

1575 Inauguration of the Theatre of Don Juan in Seville.

1577 Verses of his youth collected by Cueva in the anthology *Flores de varia poesía* (*Bouquet of Assorted Poems*) which he compiled in Mexico. Cueva sailed for Seville in the same year. Upon his return began the full flowering of his literary career.

1578 The Theatre of the Ataranzas—where several of Cueva's plays would be performed—was first used about this date. Death of the Portuguese King Sebastian in the Battle of Alcazar-Kebir.

1579 *Début* of Cueva's first drama *La muerte del rey don Sancho, y reto de Zamora* (*The Death of King Sancho and the Challenge of Zamora*) at the Theatre of Doña Elvira in Seville. Seven more plays had their première the same year.

1580 Four plays of Cueva performed in the theatres of Doña Elvira and Don Juan. Fernando de Herrera published his *Anotaciones a Garcilaso* (*Commentary on Garcilaso*). Portugal annexed by Spain.

1581 Cueva composed an Italianate song celebrating the return of Felipa de la Paz to Seville after a plague which had threatened the city subsided.

1582 Cueva published the first part of his *Obras* (*Works*)—amorous poetry in the style of Petrarch.

1583 Cueva published in Seville the first part of his *Comedias y tragedias* (*Comedies and Tragedies*), which contained all fourteen of the extant dramas.

1584 Cueva granted permission to publish his plays in a second printing.

1585 Cueva completed the manuscript of *El viaje de Sannio* (*Sannio's Journey*) which he dedicated to his patron, the Marquis of Tarifa.

1587 Cueva published his collection of artistic ballads, the *Coro febeo de romances historiales* (*Phoebean Chorus of Historical Ballads*).

1588 Second printing of Cueva's *Comedies and Tragedies* in Seville.

1590 Cueva composed funereal elegies on the deaths of his friends Diego Girón and the Marquis of Tarifa.

1592 Herrera published his translation of *Elogio de la vida y muerte de Tomás Moro* (*Praise of the Life and Death of Thomas More*).

1594 Death of Cueva's patron Fernando Enríquez de Ribera, second Duke of Alcalá.

1595 Cueva was authorized to publish a second volume of plays, none of which is thought to have survived.

1597 Death of Fernando de Herrera.

1598 Cueva lamented the death of Philip II in several elegies.

1600 Cueva petitioned the city of Seville to assume the costs of printing his long narrative poem *La conquista de la Bética* (*The Conquest of Andalusia*).

1603 Publication of *The Conquest of Andalusia* which had been begun much earlier. This same year he dedicated to his brother Claudio a manuscript copy of the first volume of his poetry.

1604 Cueva began the manuscript of a second volume of verse probably drafted over the preceding twenty years. The same year he completed *La historia y sucesión de la Cueva* (*The History and Issue of the Cueva Family*).

1606 Cueva composed his *Ejemplar poético* (*Poets' Guide*).

1607 The probable date of the beginning of Cueva's residence in

Cuenca. Completion in Cuenca of his long composition in verse *Los inventores de las cosas* (*The Inventors of Things*).

1609   Cueva probably still resided at Cuenca where he edited a new manuscript of the *Poets' Guide*.

1610   The probable year of Juan de la Cueva's death.

CHAPTER 1

The Historical Moment

I *Juan de la Cueva's Life*

SEVILLE has perhaps never produced a greater chauvinist than Juan de la Cueva. The salient feature of both his personality and his literary works is a near fanatic pride in his Sevillian ancestry. Any study which attempts to do justice to his biography must impart the extraordinary love for his city that Cueva never permitted to subside. It is cruelly ironic that so enthusiastic a voice should in time be forgotten by the very city whose glories he strove to enshrine forever. Never a modest man, Cueva took every precaution to insure that the story of his life would be as an open book to posterity. Despite such candor, his biography has been especially shrouded in mystery and confusion. Until very recently, not a few literary historians disagreed on the century during which he lived. The paradox of his zeal for fame and recognition and the apparent paucity of biographical data is easily explained. The bulk of his personal anecdotes—a virtual diary waiting to be violated—was scattered throughout many manuscripts not readily accessible. Generations of historians found it far simpler to perpetuate the inaccuracies of their predecessors than to go to sources rare among the rare.

The positivistic approach of the Swedish scholar Fredrik A. Wulff has effectively eradicated many of the misconceptions which crept into the scanty standard references to Cueva for centuries. To date his biographical treatise is the most complete and authoritative, and it is to it that researchers must revert.[1]

Seville—the "Queen of the Ocean" as Cueva's contemporary Fernando de Herrera described it—could well be proud of this native son and his distinguished family. Few more noble lived in all of Andalusia. Juan de la Cueva de Garoza was born about 1550. He grew up in an atmosphere enriched and stimulated by prestigious family accomplishments in the fields of politics, law,

17

and religion. It is clear that he rejoiced in the eminence of a kinship with the powerful and influential men who had succeeded in fostering the Renaissance attitude that placed equal glory on arms and letters. Indeed, Cueva's self-assurance and the impudent forwardness born only to the real nobility are the recurring leitmotifs of his autobiographical works.

Juan was the fifth of the eight children of Doctor Martín López de la Cueva and his wife Juana. Perusal of the epistolary poems and his apotheosizing *Historia y sucesión de la Cueva* (*History and Issue of the Cueva Family*)[2] yields intimate glimpses of each brother and sister. Close bonds of affection are evident. Beatriz, the oldest, is portrayed as a serene, prayerful woman silently suffering the infidelity of her husband. Juan was particularly fond of Isabel, whose progeny he predicts will be as illustrious as her forefathers. Francisca is described as a Christian Portia, a picture of fidelity. Though he extols the intellect of Juana, the youngest, clearly his favorite is Claudio— the ecclesiastic luminary of the family who became an inquisitor. It is amusing that Juan's vision of himself was just as pretentious: crowned with the laurel wreath, smiled upon by the Muses in all his creative endeavors.[3] The only reference to his physical appearance is J. J. López de Sedano's description of his portrait which is not entirely flattering: "stout with a large head and broad forehead, curly hair, quick-silver eyes, prominent nose, stern, rigid of mien, and a generally somber appearance."[4]

Cueva traces his family origins to Beltrán de la Cueva, for whom the Dukedom of Alburquerque was created by King Henry IV, ruler of Castile from 1454 to 1474. It will be recalled that these were crucial years which were to determine the destiny of the Spanish peninsula. Upon Henry's death, the court favorite would become an anathema, an excuse for civil war. The libelous rumors that Beltrán was, in fact, the real father of the heiress Juana—nicknamed *La Beltraneja* by her detractors—lent invaluable support to Isabella's claim to the throne. Despite the unsavory tangential circumstances surrounding the foundations of this noble house, the Alburquerque emerged only slightly tarnished. Succeeding generations did much to restore the former luster. Juan's contemporary, the seventh Duke, gained considerable renown. In 1616 this militant new Viceroy of Catalonia effectively routed the bandits, stemming the rush toward total anarchy which threatened even Barcelona.[5]

Professor Francisco A. de Icaza—whose researches have shed considerable light on Cueva's famous relatives—suggests that both branches of the family were outstanding.[6] It would seem, nonetheless, that Cueva gloried especially in the good fortune of the children of his paternal aunts.[7] Many of these cousins secured enviable positions close to the Throne. One, Andrés Zamudio de Alfaro, was Philip II's personal physician as well as a member of the General Inquisition. His son, Francisco, was knighted in the coveted Order of Calatrava, a brotherhood of elite noblemen which from medieval times had combined at once the most unimpeachable military and religious ideals. The family also included a sprinkling of decorated soldiers and jurists, even a treasurer to the Crown. His aunt, Doña Catalina de Zamudio, was a poetess in her own right, contributing a sonnet to Vicente Espinel's anthology of verse (1591).[8] Another cousin who decidedly tilted the scales to the side of letters was Doctor Luciano de Negrón. This celebrated orator, Latinist, and bibliophile assembled one of the most magnificent libraries of Seville. Doubtless Juan was a frequent browser in this repository, finding the bricks and mortar of classical learning with which to build his own altar to the ancients. Negrón eventually assumed the Archdiaconate of Seville.

Of Juan de la Cueva's personal life before age thirty, details are few. Probably at about the age of seventeen he was introduced to Felipa de la Paz.[9] He began at once to express his growing adolescent infatuation for her in amatory verse. Observing the conventions of Petrarchan love poetry, he refrains from calling her by name, alluding to her in acrostic verses or calling her by her literary pseudonym, Felicia. The first meaningful experience of Cueva's life was one of love, which of necessity could not be openly avowed. Yet his sonnets to Doña Felipa reveal sincerity in his chaste devotion to her. Cueva states in his sonnet, "My heart was held in her sweet prison" (*Fue mi alma en su dulce prisión puesta*) that they met the third of May during the celebration of the feast of the Holy Cross. Professor Guerrieri Crocetti[10] picked up this statement to show that often such allusions are pure badinage, the standard stock-in-trade of the post-Renaissance poet imitating the Petrarchan paradigm. He felt that beneath the apparent, sincere expression of his passion, Cueva intended to impart a religious fatality to the occasion through the subtle comparison of the martyrdom of his heart with the passion of Christ.

The conjugation of forbidden love and restrained impulses was a common but usually transient phenomenon in the lives of scores of sixteenth-century poets. In Cueva it persisted, no doubt his eroticism retaining to the end its adolescent naïveté. If his epistle to Zamudio de Alfaro can be believed, he pined for nearly ten years.[11] In other poems he reaffirms the commitment to resist the charms of any lady other than the beloved.

The summer of 1574, Cueva sailed from Seville for Mexico.[12] Accompanying him was his younger brother Claudio, who had recently been ordained in anticipation of an ecclesiastic career. The precise motive for Juan's journey has never been established. His brother was traveling to Guadalajara to assume the post of Archdeacon. Juan doubtless remained in his brother's company until the decision to return to Seville was made in 1577.

Nostalgia for his beloved Felicia dominates the love lyrics of the Mexican sojourn. The sonnet "Sailing safely on Neptune's Waves" (*Entregado a las ondas de Neptuno*)—dedicated to the admiral of the convoy which would return him to Spain—overflows with the anticipated joy of reunion with Doña Felipa.[13] There is also an undercurrent of a premonition of the futility of his obsession with her. Although the reconstruction of a precise chronology of his sonnets is risky, a partial linear movement is discernible. In those written doubtless upon his return, Cueva hints at the gradually extinguishing affection of the beloved. Deliberately he obscures the details of the imminent rupture of their relationship, but he never fails to maintain the characteristic tone of modesty and decorum. He masks his mortification with a façade of classical allusions which make the extraction of autobiographical data suspect. In a small body of sonnets, Cueva laments Felicia's change of heart and, eventually, total rejection of him. In several he mentions her marriage.

Attention should be called to a minor controversy concerning Cueva's conjectured "other love." Professor Wulff denies that the poet ever loved any other than Doña Felipa de la Paz.[14] Professor Adolphe Coster later repeated the rumors of an affair during his declining years with a certain Brígida Lucía de Belmonte.[15] His theory, as well as the assertion that her death drove Cueva to end his days a recluse in Portugal, remains unsubstantiated. There is no evidence that Juan de la Cueva married or that he had any issue.

Not all of the poetry written during the Mexican residence is amatory. Cueva produced a substantial number of rhymed epistolary chronicles of his impressions of New Spain. Upon the slightest pretext, he would fire off lengthy commentaries to his relatives and friends still in Seville.

These works suggest that Cueva found his personal value in the contention within him of two incompatible wills, one that of the carefree soul having at last found liberty, and the other that of the homesick wayfarer beset with ennui. The psychological pendulum swings first one way and then the other. Exuberantly he urges his correspondents to cast off the fetters of urban life and join him in an unspoiled terrestrial paradise. His panegyrics continually echo the Theocritan eulogy of the simple life. His appreciation of the silence of this tranquil land is eloquently stated in the verses of the epistle, "A single moment slips by, a single breeze" (*Un tiempo corre solo, un solo viento*).

It was not long before Cueva's social conscience was aroused. His fifth epistle—addressed to the Corregidor of Mexico—describes the living conditions of the Indians and cries out for injustices and oppression to be alleviated.[16] These compositions—so long virtually unknown—contain the seed of Cueva's future lyric. It is far easier to condemn a work than to read it. Cueva's detractors would have been well advised to search for the moral dimensions of these early compositions rather than dismiss them as unworthy of their consideration.

Cueva's delight in the natural primitivism of Mexico was short-lived. The sweet nectar of peace and well-being turned to gall. He became the malcontent, reliving in the epistles his memories of home, longing for the return to Seville. As his boredom increases, spirtual anxiety grows. Before packing his bags for the now eagerly-awaited repatriation, Juan penned the first known collection of verse to appear in the New World.

The *Flores de varia poesía* (*Bouquet of Assorted Poems*) contains—in addition to Cueva's compositions—representative works
of thirty Spanish and Creole poets. Cueva's distinction of being
America's first anthologist was disputed by Icaza.[17] He argued
that in view of the date of the manuscript (1577), Cueva would
probably not have had sufficient time to copy such an extensive
body of poems before his departure early in the year. More
recently, the controversy attracted the attention of Professor
Renato Rosaldo, who favors Cueva as the probable compiler
of the codex.[18] He includes several of Cueva's sonnets in his
anthological edition of this work.[19]

Juan de la Cueva was later to make an even more decisive
impact on Mexico. Once his dramas became widely known, they
were among the most popular and often-requested works to be
imported into New Spain. Professor Irving A. Leonard pointed
out that as the trend away from the reading of novels and
towards a preference for drama became apparent, Cueva's
plays were in great demand and may be considered "a presage
of the reading vogue of the seventeenth century."[20]

Cueva's true period of literary activity starts upon his return
to Seville in 1577. He was immediately reintegrated within the
intellectual and literary hierarchy of which he had been a part.
From this date his name would be linked with those of the most
noteworthy writers from Seville and all of Andalusia. He would
travel infrequently, having found in his native land an entire
moral and intellectual order with which to satisfy his occasionally extravagant inner demands. Little is known of the circumstances attendant upon his probable residence in Cuenca *ca.*
1607-09.[21] There is internal evidence in several compositions that
he visited the Canary Islands sometime after 1587.[22] Although
it is not a matter of record, Juan de la Cueva is thought to have
died about the year 1610.

II *The School of Seville*

The importance of Seville during the lifetime of Juan de la
Cueva cannot be overstated. The ancient Hispalis of the Romans,
its history was succinctly summarized in the verses chiseled into
the Jerez Gate, now disappeared: "Hercules built me; Julius

Caesar surrounded me with walls and high towers; and the Holy King [Ferdinand III] took me . . ."[23]

Seville was an intellectual Mecca as early as the thirteenth century when Alfonso X (The Wise) made it his capital. This enlightened monarch surrounded himself with outstanding scholars in the fields of philosophy, natural sciences, belles lettres, and all branches of learning. His court could rival the most brilliant anywhere in the medieval world.

For centuries after the Reconquest in 1248, Seville owed its increasing importance to its port. From wharves along the Guadalquivir River, ocean vessels sailed abroad maintaining a near monopoly of the American trade. With the Shipping Exchange (Casa de Contratación) founded there to regulate all traffic with the New World, Seville became the richest port in Spain and a boom city surpassed in size only by Naples and Paris. It was also a city of palaces, museums, and libraries of enormous value. The Archive of the Indies contains the most important collection of documents relating to Spain's American colonies. The Columbus Library (Biblioteca Colombina)—founded about the time of Cueva's birth with a legacy from the illegitimate son of Christopher Columbus—holds its namesake's rare collection as well as innumerable precious manuscripts. Many of Cueva's own autograph manuscripts are housed here.

As an irresistible magnet, the phenomenal prosperity of Seville attracted vast numbers who would gradually swing the demographic balance to the south. Some, as did Cervantes, came thinking to tap the riches which flowed through the provincial capital. Naturally, large numbers of intellectuals came and joined the cults of permanent residents. Traditionally, literary historians refer to this widely disparate assemblage of literati as the School of Seville. Great caution must be exercised in referring to any such "School." Essentially a pedagogic aid, the term should not be construed as denoting a cohesive group unified by a single manifesto. The inclusion of so many Andalusian poets is rather an attempt to point out some rather appreciable differences between this and yet another body of writers— those who tended to gravitate toward another university city, Salamanca. The distinction is largely a matter of style, and any antithetical delineation must allow for exceptions. It is usually argued that the Andalusian writers displayed greater virtuosity, that they emphasized form over content. It is a frequently-heard postulate that the School of Seville preferred bold, rhetorical style enriched by heavy use of metaphor and mythological trappings. While such generalizations may be applicable to some writers, it is by no means a corollary that all of Cueva's contemporaries fit the mold.

Much more relevant to this study is the perpetuation of an abiding interest in Humanism which characterized Seville's contribution to the intellectual growth of the Spanish peninsula in the sixteenth century. The fundamental assumption of Humanism is that man is capable of solving intellectual problems. Interest in human life as it is lived is paramount. While it may be argued that this is just the opposite of theology, Humanism did not unconditionally preclude a theological solution to man's problems. Humanism could, indeed, lead man to God. Despite her natural geographic insularity, Spain was unable to bar the gates against such heterodoxy. In time her contacts with the Netherlands introduced new concepts, not all of which were in the strictest accordance with traditional canons of faith. Erasmus of Rotterdam could not be prevented from leaving the mark of his reform movement on the face of Spain. It is not, however, the ideological import of Humanism that so greatly affected Seville, whose poets remained essentially orthodox. Here, as in the rest of the country, it was another consequence that would make its impact felt.

During the Middle Ages, schools and universities were largely dominated by the Church and Scholasticism which together imposed the rigid curriculum of the Seven Liberal Arts—grammar, logic, rhetoric, arithmetic, music, geometry, and astronomy. Not until challenged by the Humanists would the course of study evolve to become the four colleges of Arts, Theology, Law, and Medicine. Seville's free thinkers exemplify the pattern for such foundations destined to raise educational standards. Following the example of Cardinal Cisneros—whose decision in 1506 to found the University of Alcalá set the movement in motion—numerous enlightened men of Seville opened schools that were essentially secular. Thus in Seville, as elsewhere in Spain, Humanism was largely felt in the realm of scholarship—particularly interest in philology—and would prove to be predominantly of a professorial and technical nature. From the outset of his career, Seville's most famous teacher—an occasional mentor of Cueva—fostered the ideals of the new learning.

Juan de Mal Lara (1524-1571) was still teaching during Cueva's youth.[24] The highly-acclaimed School of St. Thomas, which he founded, was one of several private institutions available to students in Seville. Mal Lara surrounded himself with the most promising men of his epoch, among them the famous scholar Francisco Lucas, author of the *Arte de escribir* (*Art of Composition*). Interest in educational norms continued, but seems to have reached a crest by 1594. Guerrieri Crocetti reports that in that year the city council investigated the reason why the Humanist Nebrija's famous *Castilian Grammar* (1492) was no longer a required text in the municipal schools.[25]

Mal Lara's somewhat indirect influence on Cueva is best assessed in the similarity of their purposes. His goal in life was always self-knowledge and the transmission of culture. In all likelihood, it was he who introduced Juan de la Cueva to the writers of the Italian Renaissance.

Mal Lara wrote of his formative years in his *In Aphtonii progymnasmata scholia*—a work in which he disseminated the teachings of the great Valencian Humanist, Francisco Escobar. Much of his dynamism derives ultimately from the variety of his educational circuit which included tutelage under several Humanists of Salamanca—Francisco Sánchez de las Brozas (El Brocense) and the noted scholar of Greek, Hernán Núñez. Mal Lara's Humanism was channeled toward the cataloguing of the sum total of man's popular wisdom. His major work, *Filosofía vulgar* (*Folk Philosophy*), is an annotated compendium of Spanish proverbs, adages, and maxims which in its organization resembles the *Adages* of Erasmus. All his works—treatises on grammar and rhetoric, translations of classical authors, epic poems—express his confidence in the inherent worth of mankind. Of his lost dramas, more will be said later.

About the year 1548, Mal Lara returned to Seville from his studies at Salamanca, Alcalá, and Barcelona. He founded the celebrated School for Humanities and Grammar (Escuela de

Humanidades y Gramática) which was situated near what is
today the Hercules Mall (Alameda de Hércules).[26] Supported
by the literati of Seville and environs, the center flourished. Coster speculates that the meetings at the school were continued
after hours in the pleasant surroundings of Mal Lara's own home.
These gatherings, more social than not, constituted an informal
literary academy which functioned without parliamentarian rules
or procedures.

Here was an opportunity for the novice and accomplished
poet alike to discuss theories, read manuscripts, and engage
in mutual criticism without fear of unseemly retaliation. There
can be little question but what the dual rôle as teacher and
amicable amphitryon secured for Mal Lara the right to be considered the father of the School of Seville.

As the often transient membership grew, each regular partici-
pant came to be known by a poetic pseudonym. Fernando de
Herrera chose Iolus, the gentle southerly breeze. Cueva's close
friend Don Álvaro, the second Count of Gelves, selected the
pastoral name Albano.[27] It is not known by what name Cueva
himself was known by his fellow writers. It would seem that in
time Mal Lara set aside a particular room for the reunions of his
informal academy, a museum in miniature which was decorated
with assorted antiques and collections contributed by the members of the group. Some fifteen years after the death of Mal
Lara, Cueva reports in his *Viaje de Sannio* (*Sannio's Journey*)
that the items of the "museum" were returned to the academi-
cians, possibly at the death of the widow.[28]

There can be no question that Seville's literary academies
nourished Cueva's spiritual and intellectual appetites from the
very beginning and again in 1577 when he returned from Mexico. Professor Willard F. King aptly declares that "these organ-
izations were a powerful force in the background of the cultural
scene and . . . they must be considered as important formative
elements of literary taste and in the development of poetry,
drama, and prose fiction during the period."[29]

III *The Casa de Pilatos*

In Seville, facing a quiet plaza of the same name, there stands
the House of Pilate. Begun originally for the noble house of the

Governor, Enríquez de Ribera, successive generations added Renaissance decorations to the original Gothic style. When it was finally completed in Cueva's epoch, it had acquired a magnificence of proper proportions so seldom achieved in so diverse a plan of construction spread over nearly a century. According to popular belief, Don Fadrique, the first Marquis of Tarifa, made a journey to the Holy Land in 1519, and upon his return incorporated into the design of the still-unfinished palace features of Pontius Pilate's house in Jerusalem.

Juan de la Cueva's personal life is intimately linked with the Casa de Pilatos, its noble owners, and their retinues.[30] Upon the death in 1571 of Per Afán de Ribera—first Duke of Alcalá and Viceroy of Naples—the property passed to his brother, Fernando Enríquez de Ribera. The latter's son, also named Fernando, was the Marquis of Tarifa and would have become the third Duke of Alcalá had he outlived his father. The young Marquis was the most generous maecenas of Seville during the years of Cueva's literary plenitude. It was his special joy to invite to his palatial home the poets and artists of the city, and his lavish entertainment became legend. The opulence and taste of the family is indicated by the quality of the furnishings of the House of Pilate. Pablo de Céspedes was one of the most desirable painters in the country after Philip II commissioned him to decorate the Escorial.[31] When he came to Seville, his services were secured by the young Marquis for the purpose of decorating the family home. Professor Rodríguez Marín vividly describes alternative sites frequently destined for the amusement of guests: the lovely Orchard of the King festooned with orange groves and a placid lake fed by waters which flowed from an ancient Roman aqueduct.[32]

Cueva was a frequent visitor to the home, as were nearly all the followers of Mal Lara. The sudden, premature death of the Marquis in 1590 caused only a brief suspension of activity. The long-prescribed rituals of the family were soon resumed by his son and namesake, the third Duke of Alcalá (1584-1637). This member of the dynasty proved to be his father's rival in competition for the patronage of authors and artists. Notwithstanding his assiduous service to the Crown—for which he was named Viceroy of the Principality of Catalonia—he still found time to paint, investigate the history of Castile, and distinguish himself as a scholar of Latin. His travels permitted him to assemble one of the finest libraries in all of Spain. Don Fernando hosted an informal literary academy in his home.[33] One of the most noteworthy of its members was the painter Francisco Pacheco (1571-1654), who became the father-in-law of Velázquez. It is to Pacheco that posterity is indebted for the accurate reproduction of life in Seville during these exciting years. Pacheco conceived a plan to paint the portrait of each member of the academy. In addition, he dedicated to each a eulogy in which he describes the personality and attributes of his friends. His *Libro de descripción de verdaderos retratos de ilustres y memorables varones* ... (*Descriptive Book of Authentic Portraits of Illustrious and Memorable Gentlemen* ...) appeared in 1599, and even today is of especial interest to literary historians.

As golden threads, these personages of enormous power and accomplishments pass through the fabric of Cueva's life. His devotion to this family is apparent in the continued mutual interest each shows in the other. Cueva's autobiographical poem, *Sannio's Journey*, was dedicated to the young Marquis of Tarifa who was at the time of its completion only twenty-one. Years later, at a meeting of his son's academy, Cueva would honor the heir by dedicating to him the three epistles of his *Ejemplar poético* (*Poets' Guide*).

The most reliable index of the degree of Cueva's intimacy with any one of his contemporaries is the frequency with which he alludes to the individual in his poetry. Wulff's catalogue of these names is invaluable in assessing the size of Cueva's inner circle of friends.[34] Several in particular stand out by virtue of their primacy in this hierarchy of luminaries.

The logical beginning of the list is Diego Girón (d. 1590). A Humanist in his own right, he succeeded his brother-in-law Mal Lara as head of the latter's School for Humanities and Grammar in 1571. Cueva heralds this honor in the sonnet to his friend which begins, "Well done, generous Father Betis," (*Bien puedes, padre Bétis generoso*).[35] His bent for classical imitation is evident in the particular emphasis he placed on translating, among other writers, Horace, Virgil, Seneca, and the *Fables* of Aesop. Coster suggests the likelihood that the orthographic peculiarities that characterize the works of Fernando de Herrera (apostrophe, *i* for *y* as a conjunction, *sc* for *zc* in verbs such as *conozco*) can be traced back to Diego Girón.[36] The latter's captivation with spelling changes was contagious. Cueva was soon his most enthusiastic supporter, and even urged his friends to adopt the new orthography which his own printer, Andrea Pescioni, would respect in preparing his works for publication.[37] Girón will be remembered above all else as an impartial commentator of the works of his friends. He provided appropriate selections from Latin texts for Herrera's *Anotaciones a Garcilaso* (*Commentary on Garcilaso*). When Cueva published his *Obras* (*Works*) two years later (1582), Girón contributed a preface that differs considerably from the standard public eulogy. His is a thoughtful, penetrating analysis of Cueva's poetic techniques, a preface in which acumen overrides personal considerations. Cueva returned the tribute in a moving elegy written upon the death of his friend in 1590.

No less esteemed was Francisco de Medina (1544-1615). A student of Mal Lara, he would occupy chairs of Latin at several universities in Andalusia.[38] His works were also primarily translations, but he wrote the Prologue to Herrera's *Commentary on Garcilaso*, in which he maintained the same criteria of unbiased, thoughtful criticism as Girón. Pacheco's eulogy of Medina recalls that he was a prodigy who at the age of six astounded his teachers with the eloquence of his discourse. The brilliance of his professorships earned for him the honor of being selected as the private tutor of Cueva's patron, the young Marquis of Tarifa. There grew from this relationship deep bonds of affection and respect between master and disciple. The sudden death of his former charge so wounded Medina that he permanently renounced his academic duties and went into virtual seclusion in his home on the outskirts of the city. Cueva shared this profound sense of personal loss. In condolence he offered his friend the touching elegy which begins, "When heaven in tearful sorrow" (*Cuando en lloroso sentimiento el cielo*).

IV Álvaro de Portugal and Herrera

The name of Álvaro de Portugal, second Count of Gelves (1532-1581) was especially revered by Juan de la Cueva. A grandson of Columbus, his family was one of the most illustrious of the Portuguese nobility. During the years immediately preceding Cueva's birth, Álvaro was chosen to accompany the youthful Prince Philip II to the Spanish territories of Europe in an effort to impress favorably upon his future subjects that he would soon be their new sovereign.[39]

In 1555 the Count married Leonor de Millán, whose lineage was no less noble than his own. By 1559 he had brought his bride to his residence at Gelves—just outside Seville—where she received his literary circle. Among those in regular attendance both here and at his palace in Seville were Juan de la Cueva, Mal Lara, and Herrera.[40] Here begins one of the most celebrated anecdotes in the life of Herrera—his Platonic love for the wife of his benefactor and host. This intense preoccupation became his secret reason for living and inspired much of his best poetry.

Knowing that his love for Leonor was impossible, Herrera nevertheless became more and more overt in his amatory verses, calling her by the same pseudonyms that her husband invented: "Disdainful Light," his "Star," and his "Flame." It is thought that about the year 1575—driven by desperation to seize the opportunity—Herrera sat alone with Leonor in her garden and there confessed his love for her. From that date henceforth, he was no longer afforded the cordial welcome of previous years. Except when protocol dictated the display of a specious formal hospitality, Herrera was coolly rebuffed by his beloved. Only after her death in 1581—and only months after that of her husband—did Herrera openly avow his secret passion in a proliferation of poetic laments. As a dam broken, he pours forth the details of years of restraint. His audacity is limitless in the elegy dedicated to the young Marquis of Tarifa on the occasion of his marriage in which he openly names Leonor as the object of his chaste love.

There is evidence that the romantic idyll was not so closely kept a secret as it should have been. Cueva's sonnets in manuscript include one "To a lover who persisted in an impossible courtship prejudicial both to honor and to life." Coster posited that Cueva may well have written it in an attempt to discourage Herrera's dangerous infatuation.[41]

Alarm at an irreconcilable relationship was not the only

subject along these lines that caught Cueva's imagination. He must have been thoroughly informed of the intimate details of the Count's life and of still another duplicity which threatened his marriage. In the sonnet "Love can make many demands" (*Mucho puede el amor, i mucho puede*) Cueva again urges restraint and begs his friend to respect Leonor's constancy and excuse her jealousy which is founded on her true devotion to him.[42] Cueva seems to have feared an imminent breakdown of the marriage, due in part to the Count's inconstancy which left him burdened with an illegitimate daughter.

Before proceeding further, mention should be made of what would appear to have been a deterioration of Cueva's relations with Herrera. The cause was probably Cueva's refusal to melt imperceptibly into the wave of indoctrinated poets who—with Herrera as their leader—conformed to more or less delineated poetic norms. Among his manuscript works is found an epistle addressed to Cristóbal de Sayas de Alfaro consoling him after one of his poems had been severely criticized in an academy.

Cueva reminds his friend that even Herrera's *Commentary on Garcilaso* was censured by an anonymous critic using the pen name of The Jacobin Priest. Under the pretext of offering solace, Cueva really directs lampoons at both Herrera and the anonymous critic. His indignation stems not from distaste for the literary philistine who dared to attack Herrera, but from realization of the pointlessness of quibbling over minutiae. He must have sensed that the sort of verbal splitting of hairs in which both were engaged would ultimately impoverish the acceptable poetic lexicon.[43] At any rate, his satire of one of the most powerful of Seville's poets may well have cost him dearly.

In reducing the vast canvas of Cueva's life to workable proportions, we must delve briefly into the likely consequences of Cueva's outspoken tendencies—the disappointment and frustration of his mature years. His biographers have never pinpointed the precise origins of a series of events which left the poet embittered and emotionally detached. The later works, especially, are tinged with the unmistakable imprint of depression and acrimonious allegations that he has been unjustly denied recognition for his literary accomplishments. For reasons unknown, Cueva decided not to proceed with the publication of several major works which he had already completed. Historians hint at a major rupture with his literary associates and even a concerted boycott by prominent members of the School of Seville.

In particular, two slights—involving outsiders rather than Sevillians—have intrigued scholars. First, on no occasion does Cueva mention Cervantes, whom he certainly must have known during the latter's residence and imprisonment in Seville. Yet Cervantes acknowledges him in his "Canto de Calíope" ("Caliope's Song") in the *Galatea* published in 1584. Wulff suspects that Cueva's refusal to allude—even unfavorably—to Lope de Vega probably resulted from the latter's eclipse of the Sevillian's dramatic career (p. lxvi). Conversely, it is indeed curious that Lope omitted Cueva's name from the lengthy roll of distinguished authors which his *Laurel de Apolo* (*Apollo's Praises*) comprises.

We come away from the intriguing details of Cueva's life and milieu feeling the frustration of being unable to penetrate the enigma further. At the same time, compensation for this deficiency is found in Cueva's works. Even today their message is clear. Despite whatever abuse or malignity he suffered—or imagined he suffered—he never lost faith in himself and the ideals by which he lived. In the pages that follow, we shall see these concepts emerge from his works which are, after all, the *summa* of the man.

CHAPTER 2

Cueva's Dramatic Art

THE reputation of Juan de la Cueva has rested almost entirely on the assumption that he was a precursor, if not the founder, of the Spanish national drama, which—in the hands of Lope de Vega—reached maturity in the early seventeenth century. Echoing his own far-reaching claims of dramatic innovation in the *Ejemplar poético* (*Poets' Guide*), hispanists have perpetuated this contention without adequate critical verification. In modern times students of the Spanish drama have fallen into serious disagreement over the legitimacy of such claims. Yet, understandably, in the absence of a satisfactory and convincing explanation of the sudden, unprecedented evolution of Lope de Vega's dramatic formula, they continue to revert to the traditional clichés. The history of the Spanish theatre can never be fully understood until underlying misconceptions are corrected and Cueva's dramaturgy is put in a proper perspective. His contributions are best appreciated when compared with those of his predecessors and contemporaries. To this end there follows a schematic survey of landmarks in the drama with particular reference to Seville.

I *The Neoclassical Tradition in Seville*

It is a fact now generally accepted by hispanists that the origins of the drama are to be sought in the Christmas and Easter tropes—interpolations in the liturgy which were expanded to contain secular material. It is also believed that the Spanish drama spread south and west from Barcelona and Valencia to other provincial municipalities. Professor Shergold reminds us that by the sixteenth century Seville had assumed a position of preeminence in the performance of the *auto sacramental* (plays performed during Corpus Christi festivals to promulgate Catholic dogma).[1]

The secular drama had also attained a degree of complexity

33

far removed from its humble origins. Basically it had followed three fundamental lines of development: the nativity and Virgilian pastoral modes as conceived by Juan del Encina and his imitators; the imitations of Torres Naharro and the combinations of romantic comedy with motifs borrowed from the *Celestina* and the Italian *commedia dell'arte*; and, third, humanistic and school drama which flourished primarily in Jesuit centers. The latter was a prescribed literary exercise designed to implant the fundamentals of classical discipline in students who sometimes performed their compositions. Periodically, there would appear fleetingly on the surface of this mainstream of drama an innovation in subject matter or technique which usually left no lasting impression in the ebb and flow of theatrical tradition. Such was the case when Gil Vicente turned to chivalric material for two plays: *Don Duardos* and *Amadís of Gaul* (ca. 1523).

It is clear that before 1585—by which date Madrid had become uppermost in importance as the theatrical capital—the Spanish drama gravitated to schools of playwrights whose associations were with provincial towns. It is difficult to establish Cueva's debt to Spanish playwrights because little is known about his immediate predecessors in Seville. Had he not himself named some of them in doctrinal works, most would probably not be remembered today. In the third epistle of the *Poets' Guide,* which treats the drama, Cueva states that the classical canons of playwriting were observed by Guevara, Gutierre de Cetina, Cozar, Fuentes, Ortiz, Mexía, and Mal Lara (vv. 532-37). Of these, only Cetina, Mexía, and Mal Lara made any lasting impression on the pages of literary history, and none is noted for his dramatic production. Cetina (d. *ca.* 1557) is remembered primarily for his poetry in the Petrarchan vein, and none of his plays survives. Yet Cueva is not alone in his praise of this writer. In his biographical sketch of Cetina, Pacheco refers to two volumes of plays, one a collection of moral plays in prose and verse and the other, secular works.[2] Pedro Mexía (d. 1551) won renown for the historical prose which he edited as the chronicler of Charles V as well as for his very popular miscellany of verse, anecdotes, and almanac data entitled the *Silva de varia lección* (1540). Of Juan de Mal Lara, more needs to be said.

Cueva's claim that his friend and teacher was the author of one thousand tragedies cannot be substantiated, since not even one has survived. Yet it is apparent that his interest in the drama began as early as 1548 when—as a student at the University of Salamanca—Mal Lara wrote a play which he called *Locusta* which was performed by his classmates.[3] The tragic themes of exploitation and betrayal—seen in the dramatization of Locusta's execution for her part in the poisoning of the enemies of Nero and Agrippina—suggest the brand of tragedy which was currently favored in the university circles.

It would appear that Mal Lara was largely responsible for the vogue of composing plays in a mixture of Latin and vernacular languages. He states in one of his lyric poems that, while a student, he experimented with plays composed in Latin and Spanish, and some have attributed to him the *Tragedy of St. Hermenegildo*, which was performed by Jesuit priests in Seville in 1580.[4] This five-act play—which combines Latin, Italian, and Spanish—honors the memory of the patron saint of the college.[5] The importance of the school drama in Seville has certainly not been sufficiently recognized.[6] Shergold reminds us that there was heated competition between the Jesuit playwrights and other dramatists who wrote mainly for performances held inside the church.[7] And Bonilla—trying to account for dramatic evolution from the time of Encina to that of Cueva—mentions humanistic comedy in Latin and the school drama as uppermost in the trend towards classical imitation.[8]

It is clear that Cueva's dramatic formula was in large part shaped by the Renaissance interest in translation and philology. Likewise, the discussions of dramatic precepts which were hosted by Mal Lara were certainly no small factor in determining the direction which Cueva's dramatic experiments would take. Cueva states in the *Poets' Guide* (III, vv. 697-99) that Mal Lara was responsible for modifying the existing drama and making it more compatible with contemporary interpretations of classical theory.

Since Cueva's classical imitations are most apparent in the tragedies, it is useful to review briefly the relative successes and failures of this genre in Spain before Cueva tried his hand at it. Alfredo Hermenegildo's recent survey of sixteenth-century

Spanish tragedians[9] promised to elucidate a zone of investigation often clouded by misconceptions. Unfortunately, this lengthy book is so marred by inaccuracies and sloppy redaction that its usefulness is marginal—the Cueva bibliography alone contains nearly a dozen errors.

The conceptual basis of classical tragedy never really flourished in Spain. Catholic dogma of free will rejected the *fatum* upon which Greek and Roman tragedy were based. The sporadic attempts to awaken Spanish interest in tragedy during the sixteenth century were marked by compromises of strict classical theory. While some formal elements—such as composition in verse and symmetrical division of the action into five acts—were usually retained, others were just as often ignored. Thus it is that the unity of time was not always insisted upon, and the plot might produce a social equilibrium with characters drawn from the proletariat rather than exclusively from the nobility. As might be expected, there was rarely any trace of the chorus.

The first appearances of tragedy on the Spanish peninsula were translations or very faithful adaptations of specific Greek and Latin models. For example, the Andalusian Hernán Pérez de Oliva (1494-1533) translated into prose two important plays: Sophocles' *Electra* which he called *La venganza de Agamemnón* (*Agamemnon's Revenge*) and Euripides' *Hecuba* which he entitled *Hécuba triste* (*Hecuba's Melancholy*). He also translated Plautus' comedy *Amphitrion*.

By Cueva's lifetime the impetus provided by Humanism had been channeled and transferred beyond the occupation with mere translations of the classics. Dramatists including Jerónimo Bermúdez, Rey de Artieda, Cristóbal de Virués, Lupercio Leonardo de Argensola, and even Cervantes were actively engaged in enriching the vernacular literature with their own precepts for tragedy which admitted varying degrees of freedom from classical tenets. The writing of tragedy reached a peak at just about the same time that Cueva's dramas were being performed, roughly between 1577 and 1585.

Bermúdez considered himself to be the first Spaniard to write original tragedies. His two surviving works, the *Nise lastimosa* (*Suffering Nise*) and *Nise laureada* (*Nise Rewarded*), brought to the stage the story of the execution and posthumous redemption of Inés de Castro. Both plays were published in 1577 under the pen name of the author, Antonio de Silva. Both retain more formal elements of classical tragedy than do most of the others of the same period: five acts and two choruses, and the dependence on rhetorical devices such as stichomythia.[10]

The Valencian Andrés Rey de Artieda departs from strict observance of classical precepts in his four-act tragedy, *Los amantes (The Lovers)*, which was published in 1581. The protagonists of this drama—which treats the popular legend of Diego de Marcilla and Isabel de Segura, Spain's thirteenth-century counterparts of Romeo and Juliet—are neither noble nor real-life heroes. A story by Boccaccio is the probable source of this tragedy in which other liberties with classical theory are also taken: the episodes are reduced to exposition in four acts in which a multitude of minor characters contribute to the blending of the tragic and comic moods.

The two surviving tragedies of Lupercio Leonardo de Argensola both have Plautine titles—*La Isabela* and *La Alejandra*. The playwright seems to have limited the action in an attempt to respect the unity of time. In discussing these plays, Crawford observes that the influence of Seneca is uppermost and that "while Argensola was not a strict classicist in his conception of tragedy, he had little sympathy with the Spanish popular drama."[11] In all probability, Cueva's tragedies preceded those of Argensola.

What has been said of Argensola holds true for Cueva. He went even further in relaxing the demands imposed on tragedy by the neo-Aristotelian canons. He allowed himself even greater liberties than those taken by his contemporaries in the matter of time and unlocalized settings. Cueva felt that the Spanish drama could best be elevated by a selective, eclectic process, one which would encourage a synthesis of the traditional free form of Spanish drama and isolated details of the classical method.

Noteworthy among efforts to define Cueva's pseudotragedies is an article by Professor Edwin S. Morby,[12] who remains today the authority on Cueva's tragedies. He judiciously writes that the most pervasive influence on the playwright is that of Seneca, and goes so far as to say that Cueva was, in fact, the first to introduce Seneca on the Spanish stage. What is more, he states, "In both tragedies and comedies it is the *sole* influence exerted on him by classical tragedy" (p. 384). It is worth recalling those features of Senecan tragedy which this scholar finds heavily exploited by Juan de la Cueva: sensationalism manifested in the grotesque and the horrible (for example, unusual methods of torture and execution); magic and the supernatural, with a preference for infernal apparitions; omens and forebodings; rhetoric, usually expressed in sententious monologues and bombast; philosophical lyric tirades; a fondness for perverse characters; and, finally, the repeated use of the motif of vengeance. Professor Morby observes that revenge is the principal motif in nine of Seneca's ten tragedies, while more than half of Cueva's plays depend on the same motif for the main action.[13]

In his enlightening consideration of Cueva's dramaturgy, Professor Morby recognizes that the tracing of influences is often a risky undertaking and is subject to possible false attributions. It may well be that the gap between Seneca and Cueva was not bridged directly, but by intermediary Italian versions known and imitated by the Sevillian playwright.[14]

The same observation holds true for the sources and models of Cueva's comedies, which are not so easily identified as one might imagine. Cueva drew freely from the common wellspring of Italian plays and reworkings of Latin plays which nourished earlier generations of Seville. Raymond L. Grismer states that there was a large school of Plautine imitators in Seville early in the sixteenth century.[15] Likewise, the works of many Italian writers—including Cecchi, Raineri, Secchi, Rhodigino, and Ariosto—who exploited many classical romantic motifs were widely known and imitated in Spain. Cueva's humanistic bent permitted manifold borrowings, and although he boasted that he owed nothing to Euripides, Menander or Terence,[16] one can isolate technique and motifs clearly borrowed from Virgil, Ovid, Livy, Lucian, and others.

Cueva, more so than any of his contemporaries, led the way in establishing a dramatic formula that would combine the best of the classical traditions and the native Spanish tendencies. He saw no difficulty in stretching the time represented in the course of a single play far beyond the limits allowed by Aristotle. He expanded upon the standard uses of narrative monologue, making of it a convenient vehicle to describe action that has not been seen on stage. He adopted the new preference for a four-act division of the action. And, following the custom of his predecessor Torres Naharro, Cueva termed each division a *jornada* (the events of a single day).

The question of generic nomenclature is sometimes considered problematic insofar as the history of Spanish drama is concerned. Juan de la Cueva specifically called four of his plays "tragedies" and the remaining ten, "comedies." This is not to say that these distinctions were determined by the restrictions on content imposed by Aristotle's theories. Cueva combines in a single play the tragic and the comic, the highborn and the peasant. Furthermore, his tragedies do not always conclude on a disastrous, gloomy note, nor do the comedies exclude calamities. In fact, deaths occur in all but one of his plays. As Lope de Vega would learn to do after him, Cueva made generic distinctions which were determined primarily by the subject of the play rather than by the form in which it was presented. Cueva chose as subjects for tragedy those whose sources claimed at least a foundation of historical truth. These include such true-seeming variants as pseudohistorical legends (i.e., the play based on the history of the seven Infantes of Lara).

Juan de la Cueva is responsible for still another innovation which, in time, would become a distinguishing characteristic of the national drama—polymetry. One of the first to consistently employ strophic variety in his plays, Cueva was also the first to mingle both native Spanish and Italianate meters. This practice of strophic flexibility had been briefly tried by Gil Vicente, whose experiment did not meet with any degree of success. It was left to Cueva to demonstrate that different meters would be most effectively used when adopted for certain situations and character types.[17]

Cueva's metric variety includes the following kinds of strophes: the *redondilla* (the only native Spanish strophe used, which accounts for more than half of all the verses), and the following Italianate forms: the *estancia*, the tercet, blank verse, and octaves. It is interesting to note that Cueva, unlike Lope de

Vega, scorned the traditional ballad strophe which he employed only in the *Coro febeo de romances historiales* (*Phoebean Chorus of Historical Ballads*). He apparently felt that so lofty an enterprise as the drama should not be debased by so mundane a form of verse. Cueva persisted in this attitude and felt especially justified in his snobbery when Lope de Vega carried the *romance* meter to great artistic heights in his own plays.

Mention should be made of the length of Cueva's plays. They are nearly one-third shorter than the standard seventeenth-century *comedia* which averages between 3,000 and 3,500 lines. Cueva's fourteen plays average only two thousand lines, but there is great disparity among them. The shortest, *La muerte del rey don Sancho y reto de Zamora* (*The Death of King Sancho and the Challenge of Zamora*) contains only 1,312 lines, while *El viejo enamorado* (*The Old Man in Love*) is more than twice as long (2,690 lines). Even within a single play Cueva tends towards acts of unequal length, some consisting of fewer than three hundred lines while others exceed seven hundred. Doubtless the opportunity for expanded plots afforded by fictional motifs accounts for the fact that the six novelesque plays are among the longest. These average 2,350 lines.

It was the custom in the sixteenth century to include a variety of prefatory material before the play proper. The prologue, or *introito*—intended as a short introductory speech spoken by one of the characters—was often a means of getting the attention of the audience which was notoriously disorderly. At a later period of development it was called the *loa*. Often short prose summaries of the plot (*argumento*) were included to be read before each act. Cueva completely stripped his dramas of these externals. The general prose summaries which precede each play and the shorter condensed versions before each act appear only in the second printing of 1588. Apparently, these were intended for readers at home and not to be recited on the stage.

Cueva set great store by the formality of his plays, which he viewed impersonally, with almost no link to his private life. This is, perhaps, the most marked dissimilarity between his dramaturgy and that of Lope de Vega. It will be remembered that the personal anecdote, the lived experience, is the leitmotif of Lope's entire career as a playwright. Obsessed with his own amorous adventures, he extended the masquerade to its ultimate limits, introducing himself and his mistress in his plays while dramatizing, again and again, specific episodes from his own experience. His life experiences became such a vital part of his opus that it is often difficult to determine in a given work where reality leaves off and fiction begins. One looks in vain for the least hint of personal involvement or emotion in the plays of Juan de la Cueva.

In its structural apparatus, the Cuevan play again betrays the influence of Seneca. Professor Morby finds that "in the construction of his plays, he underwent a distinct evolution that brought him ever closer to the tragic mold."[18] He goes on to say that, abiding by the dictates of classical theory, Cueva begins his plays with the exposition—the introduction of the initial situation and the characters who will be involved in the resolution of the dialectic. Cueva's most often-repeated technique is the presentation of the exposition in a monologue or a dialogue between master and servant.[19] Furthermore, by the time Cueva had completed his fifth play, *El degollado* (*The Beheaded Man*), the figures of both a true protagonist and antagonist had emerged. Once established, Cueva maintains a consistent form which allows a linear movement in the development of the plot—exposition in the first act, the momentary victory of the antagonist over the protagonist in the second act, the climax and forecast of victory for the antagonist in the third act, and, finally, in the fourth, the working out of the catastrophe and the use of a *deus ex machina* to restore the advantage to the protagonist.[20]

Finally, any meaningful reading of Cueva's plays must take into account his forensic oratory. A science which was understood and practiced by sixteenth-century writers almost to a man, it is the essence of Cueva's dramatic style. In order to condition the audience to accept a prescribed moral view, the dramatist relies upon a whole battery of devices of rhetoric, the art of persuasion, Cueva manipulates language in order to put his audience in a more receptive frame of mind. The fact that there is more declamation—characters speaking *at* each other rather than *to* each other—than dialogue should not lead to the condemnation of his language as unnatural by the modern reader.

His plays abound with passages of high-flown, pretentious eloquence which, as the language of Shakespeare, struck the listener and forced him to savor the lines.

Naturally, the possibilities of rhetoric are almost without limit. It can be employed to invoke a multitude of emotions in the listener: anger, pity, horror, fear, confusion, etc. In addition, the threefold means of persuasion basic to neo-Aristotelian rhetoric (*logos, pathos,* and *ethos*) can be further divided into more than two hundred figures of speech which are readily incorporated into the poetic language. Cueva was fully cognizant of the dramatic potential for persuasion inherent in these figures and made the best use of them. The result is that his plays, more so than those of any of his fellow dramatists, can only be fully appreciated when being read aloud or seen performed. His artistry derives from, and is entirely dependent upon, the spoken word. It would be a herculean task to sift from Cueva's plays the sum total of these figures of speech. One can discover, fairly readily, that Cueva's rhetorical strategy depended more heavily on some devices than on others. For example, the most often repeated is the device of repeating the same word, or a close derivative, in different forms and contexts. The effects are primarily rhythmic and alliterative, as the following examples from *The Seven Infantes of Lara* illustrate:

> My obligation to obey you
> is so uncompromising that it demands
> that I must necessarily do
> whatever should be required to humor you.

> (*La fuerza de obedecerte*
> *es de tal fuerza que esfuerza*
> *a que se haga por fuerza*
> *lo que fuere complacerte.*)

> I cannot imagine how I shall be able
> to allow you to be on your way,
> nor how you will have the courage
> to say goodbye.
> But the motive which governs
> with such urgency your departure

concedes the stamina which is needed
by my life which will be one of suffering.

(*No sé como pueda darte*
licencia para pedirte,
ni tú para despedirte
cómo puedes esforzarte.
Pero la causa que fuerza
con tal fuerza tu partida
esfuerzo dona a la vida
que para penar se esfuerza.)

Clearly, any attempts to render the subtleties of the original language in translation are doomed to failure, and demonstrate, once again, how inadequate is any literary interpretation based on any text other than the original.

As we have seen, Juan de la Cueva's dramatic formula was governed by impulses from an extraordinarily rich, constantly present Renaissance-humanistic erudition. To return to the fundamental question of his influence on Lope de Vega's dramatic art—and by extension, on the *comedia* in general—an often-made claim must be refuted. The assertion that Cueva's introduction of Spanish history and national heroes on the stage paved the way for Lope's dramatization of the same material is specious. Certainly, Cueva exploited national legends in his first four plays. That he should write no more on Spanish history and should turn instead to other sources would suggest a probable repudiation of his first choice. Once Cueva turned to dramas based on classical history and novelesque motifs, he did not return to national history.

It should also be stressed that Lope de Vega's first manner definitely was not the dramatization of historical drama. Only two plays written before 1590 can be considered historical, and only then with great reservations. *Los hechos de Garcilaso de la Vega y Moro Tarfe* (*The Deeds of Garcilaso de la Vega and the Moor Tarfe*) is Lope's earliest known play, and the only one extant in the primitive four-act form. More fictional than historical, it must be considered a youthful experiment which, once tried, was abandoned in favor of other possibilities. His

El nacimiento de Ursón y Valentín (*The Birth of Orson and Valentine*) is based on an old French romance and may be considered semihistorical. However, it is related to the story of King Pepin and thus is connected not with Spanish history, but with the Carolingian cycle.

To reiterate, although Lope turned to history and semihistorical legends for dramatic inspiration in the plays of his mature years, his emergence as a dramatist is in no way tied to the precedent established by Juan de la Cueva. Other unrelated influences were brought to bear on Lope so forcibly that they would characterize not only his early, but his mature dramas as well.[21] The failure to perceive the divergence of these two essentially different dramatic dialectics led Guerrieri Crocetti to conclude that Cueva was, in fact, responsible for the establishment of the Spanish national theatre.[22] His thesis is simply not tenable.

Obviously, this conclusion leaves the all-important question of the significance of Cueva's drama unanswered. Viewed in depth, the significance of Cueva's drama is not to be sought in its historical transcendence, but in its intrinsic artistic merit. Cueva's drama is unquestionably complex, a theatre of ideas and probing moral attitudes. His education implanted in him extremes of culture which lie at the core of his artistic power. There can be no doubt that Cueva sensed that his works would find destiny in the hearts of men who shared his intellectual heritage. Awareness of this fact is a relatively recent development in the history of Spanish literary criticism, and is only now gaining momentum.

Bruce W. Wardropper—one of the first to appraise Cueva's work as art and insist that it be judged outside its historical context—finds that Cueva's "dramatic poetry is consistently on an intellectual level superior to romance sources."[23] More recently, the late John W. Battle discovered in Cueva's plays both artistic unity and deep moral dimensions.[24] Professor A. I. Watson—guided by a more positivistic approach—has discovered political allegory in many of the plays which make them more noticeably the products of the precise historical moment during which they were conceived.[25] His theory is discussed at greater length in the succeeding chapters in which each play is afforded careful scrutiny.

II   *Stagecraft in Seville*

Juan de la Cueva's *début* coincides with a decisive phase in the evolution of stagecraft in Seville. A brief sketch of the landmarks is helpful. The earliest known plays were performed indoors within the atrium of a church or a room in a private residence. Long after the drama was moved outside the church, there was no regularly constituted or permanent stage in the modern sense. Performances were held in the open air in courtyards and public squares. Some traveling theatrical companies possessed mobile platforms mounted on carts which could readily be towed from town to town, but no city in Spain could boast of a permanent stage before 1560.[26]

The name of Seville's most famous impresario, Lope de Rueda, is inextricably linked with the growth of professional drama in that city until his death in 1565. We are told that Rueda's rise to prominence was a direct outgrowth of his direction of *autos* in Seville about the year 1542.[27] Together with his small company of players—working under the most primitive and rudimentary conditions—he performed works derived from the Italianate repertory. Shergold explains that, in the absence of court patronage for drama during the reigns of Charles V and Philip II, there was no money available for expensive experiments in settings and decorative effects. Consequently, Rueda was forced to draw almost entirely from the tradition of religious drama of the time in staging his works.[28]

The interim comprised of the years between Rueda's death and Lope de Vega's rise to prominence saw still another development. There appeared in Spain at this time a growing influx of Italian troupes whose repertories drew almost entirely on the *commedia dell'arte*. The first major Italian impresario to direct plays in Seville was Alberto Naseli whose stage name was Ganassa.[29] Favored by the powerful Gonzaga family, he had acted in Paris before being invited by Philip II to perform in Spain in the year 1574. The following year, he made his first appearance in Seville. The importance of this and similar companies cannot be stressed too much. To them is due the formation of a mass public that would be willing to pay seemingly exorbitant admission prices to view theatrical performances. Under pressure from Ganassa, the theatrical calendar was expanded to permit performances any day of the week. In his penetrating study of Italian influences on the Spanish drama of this period, Professor Arróniz remarks that these companies constitute the sequel to the earlier Italianizing wave, manifested in theory and imitation. In his words, this second wave is "not merely Italianizing, but Italian, designed to lay the foundations of professional drama through the coalescence of a resident public and the construction of permanent theatres, capable of meeting all the demands of elaborate staging and even more ambitious technical effects."[30]

Several years before Cueva's dramatic *début*, just such permanent stages were erected in Seville. Two of them were called orchards (*huertas*) because they were constructed on sites formerly occupied by groves of fruit trees. The Huerta de las Ataranzas (Arsenals) was the property of Diego de Vera and functioned as a playhouse between 1578 and 1585. Two of Cueva's plays were performed here. The Huerta de Doña Elvira, the most important of the city, took its name from the neighborhood where resided Elvira de Ayala, the daughter of the Chancellor of Castile, Pero López de Ayala. It was located adjacent to the main residence of Cueva's patron, the Count of Gelves. Eleven of the plays were performed here by some of the most acclaimed actors of the day: Alonso de Cisneros, Pedro de Saldaña, and Alonso Rodríguez.[31] Only one of Cueva's plays was performed in a third theatre, the Corral de Don Juan (John's Courtyard), which was named for its owner—Juan Ortiz de Guzmán. Even at this relatively early date, Seville could count nearly half a dozen other theatres.

Unfortunately for the student of Spanish stagecraft, the precise appearance of these first theatres has remained subject to much conjecture. Shergold's recent study has done much to shed light on this question. By and large, the stages appear to have been very similar in design to those being built in Madrid about the same time and in whose later modifications Ganassa is said to have intervened.[32] In résumé, Cueva's plays were most likely performed on stages which possessed the following features: a platform with no front curtain; an actors' dressing room (*vestuario*) located at the rear of the stage proper (*tablado*) which was separated from it by a canvas (*lienço*); an upper gallery (*corredor*) which extended beyond the hangings (*paños*) which separated the sides of the stage from the spectators' area. In addition to those at either side of the stage, there were two or three rear entrances, the middle one being concealed in a niche which could be isolated by a curtain.[33] Contained in the platform floor was a trap door (*escotillón*) which was especially useful in plays that presented magical or supernatural scenes in which actors needed to appear or disappear mysteriously. This device is an essential feature of the plays of Cueva which are discussed at length in the following chapters.

CHAPTER 3

The Historico-Legendary Plays

I Comedia de los siete Infantes de Lara
(The Comedy of the Seven Infantes of Lara)

A. Summary

THE setting of the first act is the royal palace at Cordova
where the Moorish King, Almanzor, commands his captains
to recount their victory against the Christians. Patriotic exchanges
evolve into a narrative account as the eloquent Galves, himself
a Greek, reconstructs an emotional verbal picture of the ambush
and ensuing battle in which the seven brothers of Lara perished.
Almanzor is amazed to learn of the exceptional bravery of the
group which defended itself to the end despite the vastly unequal
odds. Almanzor summons Gonzalo Bustos, father of the dead
brothers and his prisoner.

Supposing that his captor plans his execution, Bustos tries
to shame Almanzor, accusing him of abusing the unwritten laws
of diplomacy and of conduct unbecoming a ruler of his stature.
In defense of his actions, Almanzor orders Bustos to read aloud
the letter that he had brought from his brother-in-law, Ruy
Velázquez, to the King. Bustos learns that his relative had
requested his death and planned to betray his sons by delivering
them to the Moors. When Bustos inquires as to the fate of his
sons, the reply is an invitation to dine with his captor. Before
he can accept, Bustos is joined by Almanzor's sister, Zayda, who
has fallen in love with him during his confinement. Though she
rejoices in his release from chains, she fears that once he is
free Bustos will forget about their love. The act ends with his
reassurances of the permanence of his devotion to her.

Act Two begins with a monologue by the general, Viara, in
which he curses the folly of risking one's security for questionable remuneration. He sees irony in an imagined parallel in his

and Bustos' treatment by fate. Whereas the latter gambled with his freedom in exchange for a reward from his brother-in-law, Viara has risen to a position of power and wealth through guile and adulation only to be shunned by his former friends. During dinner, Almanzor is overly solicitous of his guest's comfort. After offering to summon Bustos' sons, he displays their severed heads and that of their tutor, Nuño Salido. Bustos pronounces an elegiac lament over each one as he recognizes it, extols their collective valor, and concludes that their deaths could only have come about if God had willed them, since they had no match in battle. Seizing a sword, Bustos attempts to avenge their deaths but is subdued. Impressed by his courage and his grief, Almanzor offers him freedom.

The third act returns to the love intrigue as Zayda complains of her passion to a confidante, Haja. Together they invoke the spirits of the underworld to intervene and delay Bustos' departure for Salas. He enters to bid farewell and learns that she is carrying his child. As he leaves, he instructs Zayda to rear the child in her faith, and gives her half of his ring for future identification. A short monologue by Almanzor presupposes a change of setting. He boasts of his exemption from the caprices of fortune, only to learn that his sister has borne a child who is named Mudarra. Almanzor suppresses his anger and orders a celebration.

Act Four presupposes a lapse of seventeen years, during which Mudarra has been reared in Moorish society. Zayda instructs her son to seek out his father. The boy turns to the gentlemen who will accompany him on the journey and vows to reject Mohammedanism until he has punished Ruy Velázquez and his wife Doña Lambra. The setting shifts to Salas where Gonzalo Bustos confides to Velázquez his fear that misfortune might befall his son before they can be united. Mudarra reaches the city walls and his father and uncle are pointed out to him. Bustos examines the ring, then demands that his son be baptized in the Christian religion. Mudarra accedes and exacts a similar promise from his companion, Viara. Before leaving for his confirmation, Mudarra reveals why he has come to Salas, and challenges Velázquez to a duel to the death, offering exaggerated advantages to his enemy. Heeding Bustos' advice that true vengeance is best taken with calm deliberation and not in the heat of anger, Mudarra agrees to a three-day time limit. In an emotional monologue, Velázquez confesses his guilt, shows his inherent cowardice, and plans to seek shelter at his wife's home in Barbadillo. Guessing that his enemy will attempt to save himself, Mudarra waits for him on the road to Barbadillo, where he intercepts and kills him. The play ends with the death of his wife Lambra, who is burned alive inside her house.

B. *Analysis*

The legend of the seven Infantes of Lara dates from the end of the tenth century. Subsequently, the story was given literary expression in a variety of genres including ballads and longer epic poems now lost. Cueva follows most closely prosifications of the lost epic poems as they appeared in several chronicles of the thirteenth and fourteenth centuries—the *Primera crónica general de España,* the anonymous *Crónica de 1344,* and the Ocampo revision of the *Tercera crónica general.*[1] Menéndez Pidal has indicated that Cueva must have also known a more contemporary treatment of the material, the *Historia del noble caballero el conde Fernán González con la muerte de los siete Infantes de Lara* (Toledo, 1511). Although each version is distinctive in the treatment of particulars, each relates, for the most part, the same basic story which—in view of its implication for Cueva's dramatic art—is summarized as follows.

Postnuptial jousts turn into tragedy as Álvar Sánchez, a cousin of Doña Lambra, the bride, is killed by Gonzalo González, youngest nephew of the groom, Ruy Velázquez. In the absence of her husband, and intent on immediate vengeance, Lambra instructs a servant (in some versions a relative) to throw a blood-filled gourd against the brothers of Gonzalo. The affront delivered, the servant runs to safety behind the skirts of his mistress, whereupon Gonzalo transfixes him through the material with his sword. When her husband returns, Lambra incites him to betray the entire Lara family. The father, Gonzalo Bustos, is sent to Cordova with a letter for the Moorish King, Almanzor. Unbeknown to him, the letter denounces Bustos as a traitor and demands that he be executed. Almanzor is content merely to imprison the envoy, but his sons are treated more harshly. Velázquez organizes a sortie against the Moors and alerts them as to his plans. When the ambush occurs, Velázquez abandons his nephews, leaving them to be massacred by Almanzor's generals. Their heads are severed and sent as trophies to the King. These deaths are avenged years later by their half-brother, Mudarra, the offspring of their father's union with a noble lady, Zeula, who has attended him during his captivity. Mudarra returns to Barbadillo where he kills Velázquez and orders Lambra burned at the stake.

In dramatizing the legend, Cueva faced the same problem which other cultivators of the historical drama would be forced later to reconcile. Epic prosifications had been treated as historical fact by medieval chroniclers whose strict adherence to the Aristotelian principle of the particularity of history and the universality of fiction could only be problematic to the dramatist. Cueva had to decide whether to attempt to reproduce past time objectively or to interpret it, reducing fact within the larger context of fiction. At the same time, he had to challenge the ancient tradition which dictated that poetry was appropriate for invention, whereas prose was the genre for unimaginative historical truth.

Cueva's answer to the problem of historical truth was to reduce greatly the material he dramatized. He attempted to make history meaningful by imposing upon it thematic patterns. As can be deduced from the summary of his plot and that of the legend, he excluded much, assuming a basic familiarity with the material on the part of his audience. In fact, the action begins at approximately the midpoint of the legend. Though the Infantes do not appear in the play, the memory of their courage and unnecessary deaths sustains the motif of vengeance upon which the work is based, and justifies the title.

By selecting memory as the principal leitmotif, Cueva reaffirms a classical precept upon which the seventeenth-century drama would be based—the tenet that the emotive process surpasses the lived experience. Aristotle had written that an artistic re-creation of life may appear more real than the actual lived moment. Cueva's dramatic art, then, is capable of perfecting nature and, by smoothing the rough edges of life, becomes superior to it.

It is not entirely clear why Cueva designated this play a tragedy since it does not conform to the prerequisites for classical tragedy. Divine providence is substituted for the concept of fatalism—the classical *fatum*—against which the protagonist is defenseless, and which ultimately propels him towards the inevitable disaster or catastrophe. Avoiding any references to the pagan ideology, Cueva carefully reconciles each disaster or punishment in terms of the orthodox principles of the omnipotence of divine will and justice. For example, Bustos' funereal lament, pronounced over each son's head, is not the usual elegiac outpouring of grief. Rather, in a series of rhetorical questions, Bustos explains that his sons have not been the victims of fate, but rather, have been called by God to His presence. He goes on to affirm that this is the only admissible explanation, for no mortal was capable of subduing them on the battlefield.

In the last act, especially, the dramatist insists that guilt, punishment, and vengeance are inextricably bound to divine providence and are not reducible to fortune. Ruy Velázquez' confession that he has offended heaven differs considerably from that of the typical tragic figure helplessly railing against inhuman forces. Mudarra is, for him, the fitting instrument of God's distributive justice: "And consequently, I do not doubt, for it is certain,/ that heaven my enemy,/ sends him as punishment/ for my crime and imprudence" (*Y así no dudo, y es cierto,/ que el cielo, que es mi enemigo,/ envía éste por castigo/ de mi yerro y desconcierto*).

It is worth noting that the violent deaths in the last act are more typical of the Senecan than the Greek tragedy, which generally rejected the bloodbath in concluding scenes. Another concession to Seneca's brand of tragedy is the inclusion of scenes in which magic, and especially necromancy, play a major part. The initial scene of Act Three—in which Zayda resorts to magical incantations to prevent Bustos' departure—is probably modeled on Virgil's *Pharmaceutrica*.[2] Cueva's abiding interest in the motif is revealed in a closer imitation of Virgil, his sixth eclogue entitled *Farmaceutria*, in which Clicia resorts to magical formulas to ensure a reunion with her lover, Menalio.[3]

Zayda's incantation is really the repetition, in a minor key, of the theme of vengeance. Her feeble and unsuccessful effort to block Bustos' bid for freedom proves that this form of revenge is both unreliable and ineffectual. By contrast, it serves to accentuate the deterministic note on which the play ends, i.e., that the bonds of kinship, the *fuerza de la sangre*, override all other forces, even magic and fortune.

In place of the classic emotion of terror, Cueva invokes that of wonder—the Aristotelian concept of *admiratio*. A succession of paradoxical attitudes, situations, and reactions both shock and amaze the audience. The fact that blood vengeance is so strong is, itself, sufficient to provoke wonder. Likewise, the spectator must have been amazed that Gonzalo Bustos does not punish his enemies himself. Perhaps the biggest mystery of the play is, in fact, why he is depicted as walking with Ruy Velázquez on a friendly stroll when his son arrives. Again, the answer is to be found in the Aristotelian treatises—stun the audience by presenting unique situations, but guard against impossible fantasy, which offends the intellect.

Cueva's portrayal of the Moors is as ambivalent as their earlier literary treatment had been. Though traditionally the enemy, the Moors had experienced a long period of coexistence as tribute-paying vassals. With the Reconquest ended, tolerance at first reigned, then gave way to persecution as the Inquisition committed atrocities in the name of orthodoxy. As early as the publication of the novelette *El Abencerraje* in 1561, the Moor was afforded an important literary concession. The anonymous author implies that there is essentially no difference between the Moor and Christian of good birth. Each is a gentleman who understands and respects the other's inherent virtue. Religious differences are held to be of little consequence, since love is the common bond. Henceforth, the term "sentimental" Moor describes this sixteenth-century literary attitude.[4] Capitalizing on this philosophy of tolerance, Cueva proceeded to create wonder and amazement as his expression of the Moorish-Christian dialectic vacillates. Remarkably, Almanzor pardons his sister for her cohabitation with a prisoner, and even frees Bustos. Yet he is barbaric in his teasing of the Christian whose desertion of Zayda is, by the same token, improper and inhumane. The play abounds in examples of first impressions proving to be false. For example, Bustos thinks that Almanzor is cruel, but he is, in fact, merciful, for he had commuted Bustos' sentence from death to imprisonment. Zayda thinks that Bustos is cruel when he abandons her, but learns that he is less cruel than she had imagined, for he does not take vengeance on his enemies.

Several novelesque motifs—introduced to arouse amazement—are also worthy of mention: rapid changes in fortune with over-confidence and pride preceding a reversal; the crossing fortunes of Viara (a steady, ascending trajectory) and of Bustos (a downward rush) as ironic counterpoints; and the dramatic immolation of Lambra in her own house rather than her execution at the stake.

Not to be overlooked is Cueva's adherence to still another tradition, the anonymous ballad to supply additional interest. Scattered throughout the play are fragments of epico-lyric ballads which Cueva picked up, to be inserted at just the right dramatic moment for development for his own purpose. This technique was to become the foundation stone of Lope de Vega's mature dramaturgy forty years later. Although Cueva's strophic preferences precluded the transfer of a body of ballad verses intact, he would frequently insert isolated verses which could easily be incorporated into strophes with consonantal rhyme, for example, the *redondilla*. Variety was always his keynote. This play is no exception, for in it Cueva effectively introduces lines borrowed from a nonhistorical ballad, the "Romance del Conde Claros." At the end of Act Three, Haja attempts to calm the enraged Almanzor, reminding him that "minor peccadilloes committed on love's behalf/ are always worthy of pardon" (*que los yerros por amores/ dignos son de perdonar*). Henceforth, this and similar adages would be transferred from lyric ballads to the drama with increasing frequency.[5]

The legend of the needless sacrifice of the seven brothers of Lara lived on long after Cueva's exploitation of it provided a new impetus. Among the most colorful expressions of the sequels are Lope de Vega's *El bastardo Mudarra* (*The Bastard Mudarra*) and the romantic revival of the material by the Duke of Rivas in his *El moro expósito* (*The Foundling Moor*). Despite the obvious significance of Cueva's version—his most famous play—it soon faded from the public eye. Literary historians did little to restore it to its proper perspective. Very recently there have appeared promising winds of change. Professor Anthony Watson's deliberate, positivistic approach to the work has led him to speculate on previously unsuspected implications of considerable import. He concludes in his study on this work that Cueva dramatized the ancient legend in such a way as to remind his audience of a startling contemporary parallel—the recent defeat and slaughter of the Portuguese army by the Moors in the Battle of Alcazar-Kebir.[6] He assembles convincing evidence that Philip II was only too pleased that the commanding general, Prince Sebastian, should perish, since his death removed him from the list of possible successors to the Portuguese crown. Watson points out that Philip II's failure to support Sebastian—his blood relative—with military assistance is paralleled by Ruy Velázquez' treatment of Bustos, and that Cueva glossed over any traditional accounts that might reduce his culpability. This interpretation is qualified with the admission that the play "is a parallel to contemporary events in a very general sense" (p. 80).

II Comedia de la muerte del rey don Sancho y reto de Zamora
(The Comedy of the Death of King Sancho and the
Challenge of Zamora)

During the second half of the eleventh century—the historical epoch dramatized—Spain was a divided land. The first ruler of the united kingdoms of Leon and Castile, Ferdinand I, was unsuccessful in forestalling the civil strife and fratricidal wars that erupted in widespread turmoil after his death in 1065. Though he judiciously divided the kingdom among his sons and daughters, none of their heirs was satisfied with the distribution. In 1072, having already stripped his two brothers of their lands, Sancho II of Castile besieged the Leonese city of Zamora which was held by his sister Urraca.

A. *Summary*

Act I: In an indeterminate setting, Sancho orders the Cid, Ruy Díaz de Vivar, to deliver a demand for surrender to his sister. It is to be recalled that Sancho—himself only a few years older than his vassal—had dubbed the Cid a knight at the age of twenty. Ten years later, the time dramatized, he is still a

loyal subject. The scene shifts to the walls of Zamora where
the ultimatum is delivered. The Princess and Arias González—
the aged baronial patriarch of the city who serves as chief coun-
selor—accuse the Cid of betraying the solemn oath sworn before
her father to defend Urraca's claim to the city. Denying partisan-
ship, the Cid departs to report Urraca's decision to defend Zamora
to the last man. Impatient that the Cid has tarried, Sancho
appears outside the walls. He is intercepted by Vellido Dolfos
who offers to show him an unguarded entrance to the city in
exchange for asylum. Despite warnings that Dolfos is a traitor,
Sancho accepts the offer. The Cid urges the King to spare the
city and honor his father's territorial disposition. Refusing to
take sides, the Cid leaves Sancho alone with Dolfos who stabs
him. The Cid returns and learns of the treasonous deed from
the mortally wounded sovereign. Dolfos eludes the Cid's javelin,
slipping unharmed into the city, although his horse is felled.

Act II: The Cid counsels the Castilian nobles to dispense with
mourning in order to take vengeance on the traitors of Zamora.
The assemblage selects a cousin of the slain king, Diego
Ordóñez of Lara, to accuse formally the city of treason and
challenge its defenders to fight in the name of honor. The challenge is delivered to Arias González who denies complicity on
behalf of the citizenry, since Dolfos had acted independently
and unbeknown to the others. Because of the defamation of the
challenge, the city elects to defend itself by sending five men
who will engage the challenger one by one. A truce of nine days
is declared to enable the Castilians to determine whether such
proceedings are allowable in accordance with the ancient
statutes (*fueros*).

Act III: Ordóñez has reported to the Castilian nobles the conditions for battle prescribed by those of Zamora. On the last day
of the truce, the Cid informs Arias that the terms are acceptable.
Citing his age as a deterrent, Urraca prevents Arias from carrying out his intention to answer the challenge himself. Instead,
Arias instructs his sons to represent the city. Ordóñez kills two
of them at once. A third son wounds Ordóñez' horse, causing
it to carry him outside the confines of the arena. In accordance
with the rules of combat—which forbid either combatant to
leave the boundaries—a judge halts the duel. The Cid intervenes

when Arias attempts to avenge the death of his sons. The verdict is deferred to the judges.

Act IV: The Cid convenes the judges. Emotional arguments on both sides threaten to erupt into open warfare. The Cid again intervenes and exacts from both parties promises to accept and abide by a compromise whereby Zamora will be exonerated and Diego Ordóñez is named victor.

B. *Analysis*

This play—Cueva's shortest (1312 lines)—was performed for the first time in the Huerta of Doña Elvira in Seville in 1579. Here, again, the dramatist's debt is to the early Spanish historians and the anonymous minstrels whose chronicle and ballad accounts of the Cid's youth kept the tradition alive. In Cueva's time, indeed still today, one of the narrow portals of the ancient walls surrounding the city of Zamora was called "the traitor's gateway." There is sufficient evidence to postulate that the murder of King Sancho and the challenge of Diego Ordóñez were the subjects of a lost epic poem, fragments of which found their way into the *Primera crónica general de España*, the prose history begun under the direction of Alfonso X (1221-1284). Cueva's treatment of the material does, in fact, agree closely with the Alfonsine account, the four parts of which were published in 1541 by Florián de Ocampo. Another historian, an unnamed monk, deserves mention because his more contemporary account —in the *Crónica najerense, leonesa o miscelánea*—was the first to utilize epic material as a source. His history, written about 1160, stops at the death of Sancho's brother, Alfonso VI, in 1109. As might be expected, Cueva's dramatization of the story is occasionally at variance with earlier accounts where minor details are concerned. His changes result from the necessity of telescoping time in order to include essentially the entire episode.

Without a doubt, the play's uniqueness resides in the fact that, for the first time to any appreciable degree, a Spanish playwright inserted lengthy ballad fragments which impart a distinctive traditional flavor to the play. Recognizing the potential of the recitation of familiar verses at the moments of greatest dramatic intensity, Cueva was able to provide a new

direction for the drama. His intuition surpasses even the novelty
of dramatizing national history. It was inevitable that Cueva—
having tapped the unexploited mines of the chronicle—should
also turn to the ballad. It will be remembered that these narrative poems were at first transmitted by minstrels. In the early
years of the sixteenth century, they were printed as broadsides
or in chapbooks. Finally, they were collected in anthologies or
romanceros towards midcentury. Usually classified according to
subject, the largest single body treats episodes from the life of
the Cid.

In this simple and unpretentious play, the Cid makes his first
appearance on the Spanish stage. Though a minor character,
he is here portrayed as a man of sensible maturity which belies
his youth. The dialectic develops from the inability to align
himself with either Sancho or Urraca, for he is honor bound
to both. Cueva allows the dramatic potential of the honor conflict to subside with the death of Sancho. At this point in the
play, the thematic pattern which unifies the disparate episodes
is seen to emerge. The Cid unobtrusively lives—and by implication elucidates—the moral principle of the work. Cueva has, in
fact, manipulated history to drive home just this point—that
human affairs must be governed by restraint. One must learn
to subordinate passion and pleasure (*gusto*) to justice and
order (*justo*). Frequent rhyming of these two words in Spanish,
and the dramatization of the ideological antithesis which they
connote, was to become a commonplace in mature drama of
the following century.[7]

The most noteworthy incorporation of ballad verses occurs
when the Zamoran guard warns Sancho that Dolfos is a traitor.
Here Cueva blends lines from several different ballads with his
own in *redondillas*, whose strophic disposition easily accommo-
dates them:

> King Sancho, King Sancho,
> Do not deny that I have warned you.
> . . . .
> . . . .
> For from besieged Zamora
> There has crept a traitor.
> . . . .

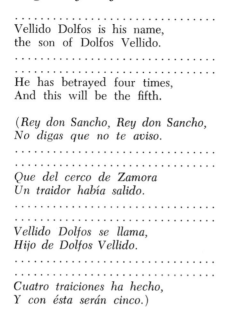

. . . .
Vellido Dolfos is his name,
the son of Dolfos Vellido.
. . . .
. . . .
He has betrayed four times,
And this will be the fifth.

(*Rey don Sancho, Rey don Sancho,*
No digas que no te aviso.
. . . .
. . . .
Que del cerco de Zamora
Un traidor había salido.
. . . .
. . . .
Vellido Dolfos se llama,
Hijo de Dolfos Vellido.
. . . .
. . . .
Cuatro traiciones ha hecho,
Y con ésta serán cinco.)

In order to provide a satisfactory conclusion to the play, Cueva had to rely on his imagination to fill lacunae in both the chronicle and ballad versions, since neither resolves the suspended Ordóñez-González duel. Cueva's originality consists of the invention of a compromise whereby both parties are satisfied, and the Cid is portrayed as mediator. He would later publish an artistic ballad on the same subject: "From the walls of Zamora,/ Arias González stands watching" (*Desde el muro de Zamora,/ Arias González está viendo*). Menéndez Pidal discusses the unsettled ending of the chronicle accounts in his fundamental study of the transmission of epic material through the centuries.[8] The thorough study of the variants in both the chronicles and ballads by Carola Reig[9] supersedes an earlier work on the same subject by Julio Puyol y Alonso.[10]

The most satisfactory interpretation of the play to date is provided by Professor Watson.[11] Arguing the case for contemporary political allegory, he finds a parallel for Sancho's lust for power in Philip II's determination to invade Portugal. Watson sees the traditional traitor Vellido Dolfos as the instrument of divine justice, "a man inspired by the most noble patriotic sentiments" (p. 51). He summarizes Cueva's intent in dramatizing the legend as follows: ". . . Cueva was asking his audience to consider what had happened in the past when a Castilian king had taken up arms against fellow-Christians. In the same play he demonstrated the advantages of judicial procedure and impartial arbitration in settling disputes where there is some doubt which party is in the right" (p. 201).

III Comedia del saco de Roma y muerte de Borbón y coronación de nuestro invicto emperador Carlos Quinto (The Comedy of the Sack of Rome and Death of Bourbon and Coronation of Our Undefeated Emperor Charles the Fifth)

A. *Summary*

Act I: The scene of the entire first act is a council of war held outside the walls of Rome in 1527. The Duke of Bourbon, commanding general of Charles V's army of Spaniards and Germans, deliberates whether to sack the city. His view that an attack is unnecessary and barbarous is unheeded. The inflammatory rhetoric of several Spaniards overrides the few dissenting votes. The arrival of a Roman messenger is announced. After being disarmed, he reports that Rome asks to be spared and offers enormous riches as ransom. Bourbon—finding justification for a rejection in the need to obey the Emperor's will—orders a predawn attack.

Act II: After a night of insomnia—and tormented by visions of Rome's destruction—Bourbon deploys the troops according to his strategy. Interrogating a Roman apprehended inside the camp, he learns that the spy had been intent on his assassination. In rapid succession, the Roman is freed, Bourbon orders the attack, and he is killed in the initial attempt to scale the walls. Having made repeated trips to their tents laden with booty, two Spanish soldiers remove Bourbon's body. A Roman matron and her two daughters flee the havoc of the city. Their determination to defend their honor falters at the approach of plundering Germans. The Spaniards guide them to safety. Offended by the sight of the Germans carrying holy objects from a sacked church, the soldiers kill the profaners in the act, then slip away with the women to avoid sharing their own booty with comrades.

Act III: Bourbon's successor, General Filiberto, is persuaded to allow the Spaniards to loot what remains of Roman wealth lest they mutiny. The duel between a Lutheran and a Spaniard is halted. Filiberto sentences the former to be drowned in the Tiber after learning the reason for the quarrel—the Spaniard's intercession on behalf of a nun in her pillaged convent. A messenger implores that the sacrilege of Rome's temples cease. Expressing his deep shame at the atrocities, Filiberto lifts the siege. The Roman also offers ransom for the three noble women held by the Spanish soldiers. They are freed after having cited the care and respect with which their captors had treated them. Drummers sound the command to proceed to Bologna.

Act IV: Don Fernando reminisces in Bologna with another Spaniard who had learned of the victory before leaving Barcelona in the entourage of the Emperor. They discuss the political expedients which prevent the coronation in Rome. The play concludes with a brief scene in which Charles is crowned Emperor of the Holy Roman Empire by the apostolic envoy.

B. *Analysis*

First performed at Seville in 1579, this play marks still another innovation in the evolution of Spanish drama—Cueva's dramatization of near-contemporary history. We may be sure that the experiment pleased the public, for despite its obvious structural deficiencies, the *Sack of Rome* was Cueva's most popular *comedia*. It is the only play that he reprinted separately (in 1603).[12]

The epoch dramatized is one of the most fascinating that Cueva could have selected. In consideration of the importance of the years 1527-1530 for Spanish international politics, a brief résumé of the historical moment is justified.[13] To recapitulate, affairs of state had been particularly demanding on the young Hapsburg monarch Charles I who, at seventeen, had inherited the Spanish throne. From 1517 until 1523 he struggled to suppress repeated insurrections—reactions to his foreign advisers, his attempt to tax the nobility, and the huge debt incurred to insure his election as Holy Roman Emperor. The victory was a hollow one. Before claiming his imperial coronation in Italy, he would have to reconcile Rome with his countrymen in Germany, whose cries for ecclesiastic reform were being magnified by Luther. To complicate his struggle, the new Pope, Clement VII, submitted to Charles's greatest rival, Francis I, after the French King captured Milan. The Spanish victory at the Battle of Pavia (1525) portended a new era of Spanish ascendancy. By the Treaty of Madrid, Francis renounced his claims to Italy and recognized Charles's claim to the French County of Burgundy. As fate would have it, Francis ill paid his captor's clemency. Renouncing the agreement with Charles, he joined the Clementine League with Henry VIII of England who was currying papal favor for a divorce from his Spanish wife, Catherine of Aragon. In 1527, then, Charles faced a renewed French threat in northern Italy. With no reserves with which to pay his mercenaries, the young ruler vacillated outside Rome. Before he could prevent it, his unpaid troops were out of control and intent only on plunder.

Cueva's turning to modern history for dramatic inspiration diverges significantly from the tendencies of earlier humanistic investigations of this vast cataclysm. Alfonso de Valdés (1490-1532)—the major Spanish exponent of Erasmian thought—had devoted a lengthy prose treatise to the defense of the Emperor. His *Diálogo de las cosas acaecidas en Roma* (*Dialogue of the Events that Transpired in Rome*) was edited five times between 1530 and 1547. It is essentially an apology for the excesses committed in the name of reform. Charles is completely exonerated, and his actions are praised as a therapeutic cleansing of a dissolute clerical hierarchy.

Avoiding the issue of papal decadence, Cueva resolves the problem of the morality of the attack on Rome by stressing the concept of the king as God's vice-regent on earth. His judgment is simply not questioned. Crawford mistakenly assessed Cueva's purpose to have been "to arouse a feeling of righteous horror at this unholy undertaking."[14] Nothing further from the truth. The dramatic tension lies not in the juxtaposition of Charles and the Holy See, but rather in a comparison of the behavior of the Catholic troops with that of the Lutherans. Guerrieri Crocetti accurately summarizes Cueva's intent as the exaltation and defense of the inherent dignity and worth of the Spaniard.[15]

The protagonists are not the generals nor even the Emperor. They are the plebeian soldiers—Avendaño, Escalona, and Farias. The perfunctory fourth act—the only time the Emperor appears —is unnecessary for the exposition of Cueva's thesis. Even its brevity (208 lines) marks it as a concession to historicity—the logical culmination of a sequence of actual events—but not as essential as the events that it frames.

The play is, in fact, a series of tableaux. And each is a refutation of the popular charge of Spanish barbarism and heresy. Just as in his treatment of epic material, Cueva here interprets history, imposing upon it an artistic pattern. His mode is again the rhetoric of persuasion. His characters declaim as often as they act. The playwright reassures the audience that beneath external appearances of rapacity and coarseness, there breathes in every Spaniard the noble *hidalgo* spirit. Cueva's Spanish soldiers are exemplary in their defense of the three ideals traditionally held in highest esteem—courage and manliness in battle, the supremacy of Catholicism, and the sacredness of womanhood.

In demonstration of his thesis, Cueva introduces several novelesque motifs drawn, appropriately, from classical antiquity. The capture and release of the Roman spy is probably modeled on Livy's account of Scaevola in the Etruscan camp.[16] Significantly, it is Avendaño who advises the Duke of Bourbon to free the spy so that he can report that the Spaniards are above punishing a single enemy: "Let them say that one of our soldiers will assail an entire army/ but together we will not harm a man alone" (*Digan que un nuestro acomete/ un campo, y no un campo a un hombre*). Likewise, Cueva's eulogy of the Spanish defense of Catholicism is illustrated by the duel between Farias and the Lutheran, with the execution of the latter for having despoiled a sanctuary. The protection of the noble matron Cornelia and the respect for her daughter's virtue may have been suggested to Cueva by Seneca's portrayal of Hecuba in the *Troades*.[17]

Professor Watson's reading does not differ significantly from my own.[18] On the other hand, he argues that Cueva further "illustrates how difficult it is to hold back an army once it has been assembled for a specific purpose, and graphically portrays what had happened in the past when one Christian community had attacked another with the aid of foreign mercenaries" (p. 201). Watson is certain that Cueva's audience would not have failed to appreciate the marked similarity between the subject of the play and the imminent Portuguese invasion.

IV Comedia de la libertad de España por Bernardo del Carpio (The Comedy of the Liberation of Spain by Bernardo del Carpio)

This play was performed at the Huerta de las Ataranzas in 1579 by the company of Pedro de Saldaña. The historical moment dramatized—the eighth century A.D.—is the most remote epoch that Cueva re-created on the stage. His characters lived during that violent age in which Moorish invaders threatened to overrun not only Spain, but France as well. The Christian reconquest had only just begun, and even ancient Castile had not yet emerged as an independent kingdom. The play is based on the familiar story of Alfonso II, the ninth successor to Pelayo—whose dynasty of warrior-kings continued the Reconquest begun in the impenetrable mountain strongholds of Asturias.

A. *Summary*

Act I: Alfonso II, "the Chaste," will no longer postpone punishment of his sister Jimena whose clandestine relations with Sancho Díaz, Count of Saldaña, dishonor him and his kingdom. Alfonso sends Tibalte to summon the Princess from her quarters, where she is found lamenting the absence of her lover. Implacable in his rage, the King turns a deaf ear to his sister's attempts to exonerate herself, and banishes her to a convent. Jimena implores her brother to exempt from punishment her natural child, the infant Bernardo, who is being reared in Asturias. Alfonso ignores her parting entreaties and turns his harsh wrath on Sancho Díaz, sending Tibalte to lure his friend secretly from his residence at Saldaña to the court at Leon.

Act II: Tibalte takes leave of his wife, Oliva, companion and confidante of the Princess. Torn between loyalty to his King and friendship, he must conceal his destination and cruel mission.

The scene shifts to Saldaña, where Tibalte is joyously received by the Count. After an interlude of one night, the pair returns to Leon. Angered by the delay, Alfonso meets the men on the road where he accuses Díaz of treason, has him blinded and encarcerated in the castle of Luna. Finally he commands that all the grandees take oaths of secrecy and that Bernardo be brought to Leon to be reared as his natural son.

Act III: The action presupposes a lapse of several decades during which Bernardo has grown to maturity. Alfonso's advanced age requires that he name a successor, but he adamantly refuses to consider his nephew as heir. Unable to contain Moorish incursions into his lands, Alfonso offers the crown to the Frankish emperor, Charlemagne, in exchange for ridding Christendom of the infidel threat. In a new setting, two of the grandees debate how they might end the years of inhuman torment endured by the Count without breaking the sacred pledge of silence. They agree to share the secret of Bernardo's identity with two nuns who have supervised his instruction, and they, in turn, will instill in the youth the desire of vengeance. Subsequently, the nobles meet Bernardo to discuss the future of Spain. Bernardo's indignation at Alfonso's offer to Charlemagne knows no bounds. With obvious pride he accepts the charge to lead his nation in defense of its borders, asking only to be allowed to confront Alfonso first. The nun Urraca Sánchez informs Bernardo of his true patrimony and urges him to free his father and assert his right to inherit. In the final scene, Alfonso contemplates proving Bernardo's martial skills by turning him against Charlemagne's advance. The youth, with his band of supporters, confronts the Spanish monarch and hints that he will supplant him if the pact with the French is not rescinded. Alfonso acquiesces and, following Bernardo's advice, dispatches a messenger to France with a letter of retraction.

Act IV: Months later, messengers from remote parts of Alfonso's kingdom report Charlemagne's repudiation of the terms and invasion of the northern frontier. The King and his nephew prepare to march after first sending messages reassuring the oppressed cities of their imminent defense. The scene shifts to the mountain pass at Roncesvalles where Charlemagne's forces are gathered. During the battle and ensuing rout of the invaders,

Bernardo seeks out and kills both Roland and Reinalte. Charlemagne laments the caprices of fortune, and the play concludes with a eulogy to Bernardo's heroism by the god Mars.

B. *Analysis*

This is perhaps the best of the dramas considered in this chapter. Balance of parts and cohesion of theme prevent the disjunction that mars several of the plays. Cueva's successful handling of the epic material is all the more remarkable when one considers the variety and contradictory interpretations of the same motifs by different authorities.

The events attendant upon Alfonso's vengeance are related—as would be expected—in histories and narrative ballads.[19] There is even evidence that Sancho Díaz' liaison with Jimena was the subject of a lengthy epic poem not now extant. Cueva closely followed the prose accounts in the *Primera crónica general*, which tend to synthesize two diverse spirits—one French and the other Spanish. French as well as Arab historians claimed that Charlemagne's invasion was prompted by the request of a Moorish governor of Saragossa for aid in overthrowing the Omeya dynasty of Abdal Rahman I. According to these accounts, the Frankish emperor penetrated as far as this city only to find his entrance denied. He is ambushed while returning to France, and the famous knights Roland and Oliver perish in the attack.

Almost simultaneously, contradictory versions were told by chroniclers and poets living south of the Pyrenees. Three historians in particular—the Monk of Silos, Lucas of Tuy, and Rodrigo of Toledo—seemed intent on discrediting French claims propagated in the twelfth-century *Song of Roland* to having liberated Spain from the Moors. Though not always in complete agreement on minutiae, they coincide in the strong feeling of Spanish national pride.

Spanish historians were probably largely responsible for the apotheosis of Bernardo as a native counterpart to Roland. The failure to identify Bernardo with a definite historical person and his ambiguous geneology suggest that he was more legendary than real—a fabulous creation born of the desire to soothe Spanish feathers ruffled by the Gallic versions of the Roncesvalles battle. In both chronicle and ballad accounts, he is portrayed as superenvironmental, a phenomenon of astonishing physical and intellectual capabilities. Some would make him the son of Charlemagne's sister, seduced by Sancho Díaz while on a pilgrimage to Santiago de Compostela. By most accounts, however, he is the nephew of the Leonese King, Alfonso II, who adopts him as his own son.

The same vagueness and imprecision which cloud the sources crept into Cueva's play in which a strict adherence to historical chronology is impossible. The Battle of Roncesvalles (August, 778) was fought long before the reign of Alfonso and Bernardo's discovery of his identify. Conforming to dramatic exigencies, Cueva once again imposes an artificial order on the scattered, ill-defined legendary episodes. Rearranging the sequence of events, he concentrates on those scenes which glorify Spanish victory and suppresses those which detract from it.

For example, Bernardo's domestic crisis—the cruel treatment of his parents—is merely a tangential feature which Cueva does not resolve. There are no resonances from a related body of episodes which includes Bernardo's capture of the fortress of El Carpio—whence his name—and his defiance of a later ruler, Alfonso III. The culmination of this famous adventure is the deception of the hero who surrenders the castle in exchange for his father's freedom, only to discover that Sancho Díaz is a corpse. Though suppressed, this material was later given dramatic interpretations by Lope de Vega in two of his plays: *Las mocedades de Bernardo* (*Bernardo's Youth*) and *El casamiento en la muerte* (*Marriage After Death*).[20]

Apart from its interest as a historical drama, Cueva's work merits special attention for the definition of the rôle of king. As has been stated, Cueva is the first playwright to give dramatic expression to the theoretical concept of the king as God's viceregent—a figure to be honored and obeyed as one honors and obeys the Creator. The play demonstrates plastically that royal justice must be accepted as a mirror of the infallible judgments of heaven. To disavow this authority is tantamount to questioning the hierarchic principles upon which the greater World Harmony depends.[21] It is precisely this postulate—that the king cannot err in judgment—that governs the action of Cueva's play and pro-

vides the unity of parts. Alfonso, himself, summarizes the degree
of veneration which, as a sovereign, he has the divine right to
demand of his subjects:

> Whether guards are posted or not,
> the royal residence, by punctilious
> right, is always inviolable, and
> even the King's shadow should be
> venerated, and the earth upon which
> he treads adored.

> (*Que la casa real, por fiel derecho,*
> *sin guardas ha de estar siempre segura;*
> *que aun la sombra del Rey ha de acatarse,*
> *y el suelo que el Rey pisa venerarse.*)

This concept is expanded upon to mold the most poignant of
the historical plays. One by one, the characters learn that a
higher authority supersedes the urgency of personal interests.
Forced to choose between loyalty to his King and sympathy for
his friend the Count, Tibalte concludes that "Rightly or wrongly,
what the King commands must be obeyed without reflection"
(*Por que debe ser hecho/ lo que a tuerto o a derecho/ el Rey
mande*). Not even the King is exempted from the awesome responsibility that his duty exacts. Cueva portrays the misogynistic
monarch as a lonely old man who would gladly exchange places
with the humble day laborer who can forget his burdens at
sundown. Alfonso must choose between personal honor and the
greater welfare of his nation. In deference to the principles of
sacrifice, he too learns to place selfish concerns below the demands of a higher authority than himself. Because he is the
King, and unaccustomed to acquiescence, this lesson is a particularly bitter pill to swallow.

The play is, in fact, really about Alfonso, despite the title
which suggests the contrary. He is the only character who appears in every act, whereas Bernardo figures in only the last two.
Cueva focuses his attention on Alfonso's monomania—the blind
obsession with personal vengeance which impairs his capacity
to function as an impartial spokesman for God on earth. His
monomania threatens to destroy the very fabric of society.
Although as a man he has a dangerous flaw, because he is King,

he must be obeyed as the symbol of a greater, perfect authority. Both Jimena and Sancho Díaz bow to his symbolic omnipotence, but—recognizing his imperfection as a man—call upon heaven to rectify his injustices. Both Acts One and Two close on this powerful theme—the voices of the oppressed, constant in devotion to the ideal, imploring God to intervene.

It is impossible not to recognize and acknowledge that Bernardo—who alone inveighs against this rigid scheme of obeisance —is no ordinary mortal. He is the answer to his parents' prayers, a hero, a mortal favored by the gods. Cueva portrays him in a dual rôle—as deliverer of his nation in the face of the enemy, but also as an alternative to the defective monarch. He must be an extraenvironmental figure, unencumbered by ordinary allegiance to authority, in order to restore harmony, the pivotal point around which all human existence was understood to revolve. Cueva was able to capitalize on the vagueness of the chronicles as to his geneology and make his dramatic function that of mankind's savior and only hope for independence.

By successfully dramatizing the conflict of personal freedom and moral obligation, Cueva took a great step forward, paving the way for future generations of playwrights. Many of the most popular and structurally perfect plays of the seventeenth century owe their prominence to the same dialectic—in particular Lope de Vega's *Fuenteovejuna* (*The Sheep Well*) and the anonymous *La estrella de Sevilla* (*The Star of Seville*), sometimes attributed to Lope.

Despite the superiority of this play over many of the others, few hispanists have directed their attention to it. In his chapter devoted to the historical implications of this work, Professor Watson discusses striking parallels between Cueva's depiction of Alfonso and the Portuguese Regent, Cardinal Henry, whose celibacy and illness culminated in a problem roughly akin to that of the Leonese ruler.[22] Watson argues that Bernardo's historical counterpart is Antonio, the Prior of Crato, who was— notwithstanding his rumored illegitimacy—favored by the third estate. Despite his uncle's fierce opposition to him, he made it clear that he would appear at the hearings on the succession, even if uninvited. It must be admitted that the similarities are more than coincidental.

CHAPTER 4

The Dramas of Classical Antiquity

I Tragedia de la muerte de Ayax Telamón sobre las armas de Aquiles (The Tragedy of the Death of Ajax Telamon Over Achilles' Weapons)

THIS play was first performed in the Huerta de Doña Elvira in 1579 by the company of Alonso Rodríguez. It is especially noteworthy as the first Spanish dramatization of a subject from Greek history,[1] and affords the modern reader a series of tableaux in which merge reminiscences of several literary re-creations of the most famous war of all times—the siege and destruction of Troy by the Greek chieftains.

A. *Summary*

Act I: Aeneas begs his aged father Anchises to authorize the family to flee the flames of Troy. Anchises agrees, thinking to save the household gods—the lares and penates—from sacrilege. Aeneas' friend Achates describes the famous scene of the old man being carried to safety on his son's shoulders. The scene shifts to Mount Ida where Anchises restrains Aeneas who wants to return to search for Creusa, his wife, who has fallen behind. Unheeded, Anchises invokes the gods to guide his son's steps. Venus Aphrodite appears and reassures Aeneas, saying that the gods will the separation of the couple. Venus delivers her prophetic monologue on the wanderings of Aeneas and his founding of Rome. Bidding him to return to Mount Ida, Venus renews a vow to protect him since he is her son. The setting shifts to the Greek camp where Agamemnon and Menelaus are preparing to sail for Argos.

Act II: While awaiting the order to embark, Helen curses Fortune for her dishonor. Andromache, the wife of the slain Trojan prince, Hector, complains of harsh treatment at the hands of Pyrrhus. Helen intercedes to prevent Andromache's

70

execution once her true identity is discovered. Agamemnon is informed by his pilot that all the maritime signs portend a favorable voyage. The priest Calchas offers up a sacrifice. Ajax Telamon complains bitterly that he, alone of all the Greek soldiers, has not been sufficiently rewarded for his heroism in the ten-year war. He insists that the only manner in which the stain on his honor may be removed is the granting to him of the fabulous weapons forged for the fallen Achilles in Vulcan's furnaces. When Agamemnon replies that this complaint must be deferred at least until the army reaches Greece, Ajax threatens to delay the embarkation if his demand is not met. Ulysses, who has been listening to the growing altercation, immediately claims the arms for himself. After a vitriolic exchange of insults, Agamemnon silences the two contenders and convokes a general tribunal to hear both claimants and to adjudicate the question.

Act III: The setting is the same locale on the following day. Agamemnon weighs the opinions of Menelaus and Diomedes, neither of whom is able to decide in favor of one of the men. He calls for a debate in which each soldier will summarize his case, and a vote by the generals will be taken to decide the winner. Pyrrhus interrupts, vehemently protesting that his father's weapons should not be handed over to a mortal. He vows to kill whichever hero is declared the winner. Ajax and Ulysses declaim in turn in rhetorical octaves. An indecisive consensus only adds to the growing discord, and Agamemnon leaves the decision to Nestor, oldest and wisest of the Greeks.

Act IV: Twenty-four hours later, Nestor likewise vacillates in his decision. Finally, invoking the aid of the gods, he listens to contradictory advice from the entire assemblage, then pronounces in favor of Ulysses. Ajax curses the Greeks for their ingratitude and falls on his sword. The suicide horrifies the onlookers who hasten to prepare a funeral pyre. The play concludes as a personification of Fame refuses to allow the flames to consume the body of Ajax which she transforms into a flower.

B. *Analysis*

This tragedy has been harshly judged because the first two acts have almost no bearing on the subject announced in the

title. The opening scene recalls the familiar second book of
Virgil's *Aeneid*: the motif of the star which signals the way to
safety on Mount Ida. The tableau of Aeneas and his family has
no dramatic purpose other than to establish a historical framework of epic proportions. After the prophecy of Venus Aphrodite,
none of the characters of the first two scenes reappears. Once
the Homeric mood has been established, Cueva proceeds in
subsequent acts to raise to the foreground the Ovidian particulars upon which the play is based. If there is a weakness in the
tragedy, it arises because the dramatist attempted to imbue a
minor episode of the war's aftermath with the same epic grandeur of the total legend.

Far from suffering from maladroitness of technique, the play
conforms to a single well-orchestrated theme. It dramatizes two
contests which are reducible to the same common denominator.
There is in the foreground the external battle over Achilles'
weapons, but 'at the crux is the polarization of intellect and
brute force. As early as his appearance in the Homeric epic,
Ajax was a comic figure, "as brave as a lion and as stupid as a
donkey."[2] He is self-assured and obstinate because of his
strength. His adversary, Ulysses, is, on the other hand, archetyp-
ally ingenious, adept at disguises, eloquent, and persuasive. There
is almost no real action in the play because it is based on persuasion, the central theme, and the outcome is heavily weighted
in Ulysses' favor precisely because of his rhetorical superiority.
The dependence on the debate structure—as well as the portrayal
of Agamemnon as an indecisive arbiter—effectively forces the
spectator to recall the larger historical outline. By stressing the
argumentative at the expense of action, Cueva cleverly suggests
the judgment of Paris in favor of Venus Aphrodite which was
the direct cause of the Trojan War.

Cueva's source for the debate orations of Ajax and Ulysses was
probably the thirteenth book of Ovid's *Metamorphoses* where
Ajax is depicted as outrageously conceited. Cueva returns frequently to this leitmotif, insisting on his blind confidence and
indignation at having to submit to a test of his superiority when
it should be patently obvious to all. Icaza observed that, although
Cueva doubtless knew the Latin sources, he would probably not
have approached the material had it not already been popular-

ized in an unusually large number of sixteenth-century editions
of the *Crónica troyana*.[3]

Professor Watson's careful sifting of the classical sources led
him to conclusions perhaps closer to the truth. He reports that
Cueva's sympathetic portrayal of Ulysses runs counter to the
tide of post-Homeric adaptations, including that of Seneca, who
was decidedly a supporter of Ajax. He observes that the Pyrrhus
episode is an interpolation not traceable to the Ovidian version.
He adduces that Ajax, Ulysses, and Pyrrhus are the allegorical
counterparts of the claimants to the Portuguese crown, i.e., Philip
II, the Duke (or Duchess) of Braganza, and the Prior of Crato,
respectively.[4] Agamemnon, then, corresponds to Cardinal Henry,
the aged regent whose decision to refer the question of the
Portuguese succession to the Cortes is mirrored in the ballot
of the Greek generals. This convincing theory—which is amply
documented—is concluded with the admission that "the parallel
falls down with Ajax's decision to commit suicide if he is unsuccessful. Here Cueva is following the traditional story, but
the number of times that Ajax *said* in the course of the play that
he will take the arms by force if they are not awarded to him must
be balanced against his eventual suicide" (p. 115).

II   Tragedia de la muerte de Virginia y Appio Claudio
     (The Tragedy of the Deaths of Virginia and Appius
     Claudius)

This play faithfully recounts an event which is alleged to
have happened in the city of Rome in the year 499 B.C. Both
literary giants of the Augustinian Age—Livy and Ovid—immortalized the principal figures in the sordid affair: Virginius, a
Roman centurion, who killed his daughter Virginia to prevent
her falling into the hands of Appius Claudius, the decemvir.
Public outrage at the scandal was a decisive factor in the disso-
lution of this body of magistrates. Cueva's dramatization of the
subject follows more closely the account of Livy.[5] His interest in
the story extended beyond the dramatic genre—as is seen in a
historical ballad which also tells of the tragic deaths.[6] The play—
which was performed in 1580 at the Huerta de Doña Elvira—
is conceived along the following lines.

A. Summary

Act I: Appius Claudius curses Love for having disturbed the harmony of his mature years. His lascivious appetite having been awakened late in life, he now pines in vain for Virginia. His personal honor and dignity are threatened. Seeing his anguish, Marcus Claudius, his trusted servant, asks the reason, whereupon the decemvir shamefully admits to his lust. Marcus agrees to attempt to intercede on behalf of his master, and seeks out Virginia whom he finds alone with her servant, Tucia, enjoying the beauty of the Roman hills. When Virginia firmly rejects the arguments of the go-between, Marcus veils a threat in his rhetoric, reminding her that his master can take by force what he requests as a favor. Appius is close behind, and joins the group to hear the rejection reiterated even more unconditionally. Bent on revenge and on satisfying his desire, Appius plans to place Virginia under his control, and instructs Marcus as to the means to accomplish his desire.

Act II: For eleven days, Marcus has watched for Virginia outside her home. Finally he surprises her on her way to the temple of Vesta. He identifies her as his slave who, as an infant, had been stolen from him. When Virginia's indignant cries of protest attract a crowd of Romans who repudiate the claim, Marcus insists—in accordance with the plan—that she be placed in the custody of his master who will adjudicate the question of ownership. While she is being led away to face the tribunal, Tucia hurries to alert her uncle and her fiancé, Icilius. The litigants approach the tribunal of Appius, who hears the claims. His decree is that Virginia must be placed in the custody of Marcus until her father can be summoned to testify. Those assembled raise a concerted voice in support of Icilius, who protests that such a ruling compromises both his and Virginia's honor. Appius relents and entrusts her to the care of her uncle while her father is in the field.

Act III: Troubled by a dream prophetic of his coming misfortune, Virginius requests an interpretation by one of his soldiers. The explanation is interrupted by the arrival of Icilius who then retells the recent happenings in Rome, and the two men return at once. Appius convenes the hearing and Virginius appears with his daughter to defend his paternity. Marcus Claudius does not deny that he is the father, but claims that the mother was his slave who has just confessed her guilt on her deathbed. Appius interrupts the ensuing brawl to declare Virginia the property of Marcus Claudius, whereupon Virginius stabs his daughter in the presence of the entire court. Bravely defending himself, he opens a path of escape through those who would detain him.

Act IV: The Roman Senate, having determined that Appius is a criminal, has jailed him and his servant. Virginius is freed and allowed to attend the sentencing during which Marcus gives a full confession of his complicity. For their crimes, Appius is sentenced to be garroted in prison and his body thrown into the Tiber. Marcus is to be hanged in public and his body quartered. The newly-appointed judges grant Virginius' request that the latter's sentence be commuted to banishment since he has acted only in accordance with the orders of his master. When the aedile enters Appius' cell, he discovers that the prisoner has already taken his own life.

B. *Analysis*

This tragedy is proof that Cueva's outlook was thoroughly tempered by the Renaissance rebirth of knowledge and the transmission of foreign culture which continued to interest his countrymen. The ancient milieu depicted in the play is one of the oldest *topoi* of Western literature—a woman compromised by her sovereign or a superior. According to Petriconi,[7] in all the versions of the story—which he traces to Herodotus' account of Gyges and Candules and ultimately to the Book of Judges— there is a political rebellion in the background. The revolt is seen as an act of personal vindication by relatives for the affront to the woman. Petriconi observes that the earliest appearance of the legend in Spain is the story of the rape of Cava, the daughter of Count Julian, who invited the Moors to invade Spain to avenge himself against King Roderick, who had taken advantage of her. The tradition was often represented in German and English plays of the Renaissance.[8] Although there is no known dramatic precedent in Spanish, Cueva's version was soon to be the model for later imitations abroad—among them *Virginia* by the Italian Alfieri.[9]

Cueva's fourth act—which has been labeled superfluous and detracting by some—was probably dictated by the desire to maintain historical accuracy. The long narrative speech of the aedile is the most important of the act since he alludes specifically to the political repercussions of the crime: the Senate has freed Virginius in a desperate effort to avert an imminent civil uprising. His family is openly conspiring and fomenting disorder in the city. Furthermore, the fourth act is essential to dramatize the transition in the legal apparatus which Appius' shame precipitated: the decemvirs have been replaced by ten tribunes, two of whom pronounce sentence on Appius and Marcus. This concession to historicity clearly justifies the extension of the tragedy beyond the catastrophe. Finally, the suicide of Appius strengthens the sense of shame and indignation. He takes his own life to avoid judgment by his peers and because of his loss of face, and not—as Hermenegildo claims—because his plans to enjoy Virginia were frustrated.[10]

Commentators consistently agree that this is the most successful of Cueva's dramas.[11] It satisfies because of a basic harmony of parts. It is well structured and is free from extraneous secondary action. Notwithstanding the obvious classical texture of every facet of the play, Cueva still manages to impose on the work an aura of native conventionality which invites associations with traditional dramatic motifs of the pre-Lopean drama. For example, the opening monologue in which Appius rails against the cruelty of Cupid has several literary precedents. Both the medieval debate genre and the early pastoral drama abound with old men who—because they boasted of their exemption from the pains of love-sickness—are made examples of by Cupid. Appius is the archetypal victim, helplessly attracted to Virginia when he saw her by chance at a festival. Because of the class difference between them, he finally sees his civic office as the means to conquer her reserve. Yet his sense of duty and right are not easily put aside. The interior debate structure is employed by Cueva to portray the vacillating opinions of the tormented sufferer as he upholds first his dignity, then his passion. Although he admits he is too old for amorous play and

his office forbids it, he ultimately proves no match for Cupid
and goes the way of his literary predecessors.

Appius is a thoroughly perverse protagonist. His callous disregard for the public good—once the die is cast—is strikingly
portrayed in the conversation immediately before Virginia is
brought before him. Appius must select one of two censors—
whose duties include imposition of norms for public behavior
and morality. His recommendation that the position be filled by
Marcus Claudius is but one of many cases of dramatic irony in
the tragedy. He remarks in the second act that he cannot understand why the Senate permits the atrocities which occur daily
in the city streets, but that "even though the Senate might
prevail, if I should have my way, I guarantee that my brand of
justice shall put everything in order." Likewise, the control which
Appius exerts over his servant and the complete submission of
the latter suggest an unnatural bondage may exist between
the two. Marcus' speeches abound in hyperbolic reaffirmations
of his complete obeisance to Appius which goes far beyond the
dedication of a servant to his master. Curiously, Cueva allows
an overt allusion to the true nature of Appius' personality early
in the exposition. When Appius broaches the subject of his
passion, he begins by referring not to Virginia, but to her father
as the reason for his discomfort, and Marcus concludes that his
master has fallen in love with him (*¿Qué me dices, señor, das
en amarlo?*).

True to his established pattern, Cueva is more subdued in
depicting the personalities of the other characters, who are left
in low relief. Each tends to fall into a stereotype. Virginia and
her family are plebeians whose understanding of morality is
not complex. She is the archetypal discreet fiancée, mindful of
the everyday risks of gossip and conjecture which can damage
an honest woman's reputation. Thus she hesitates to leave her
house, and when she does, she is reluctant to tarry on walks no
matter how attractive she finds the countryside. She knows that
honor is a very fragile commodity that can be destroyed by even
a hint of suspicion. Here Cueva anticipates the seventeenth-
century emphasis on honor that is based on reputation rather
than on conscience. The same is true of Virginius. His only guiding principle is the supremacy of reputation. His public image

as a Roman centurion is on a par with life itself. Consequently,
when he stabs his daughter, it is to prevent not only her loss
of honor but, more significantly, his own disgrace. His sense of
personal loss is obviated by the restoration of justice. Indeed,
justice is the only demand that captures his emotion. Sorrow is
secondary. It is left to Icilius, the tragic fiancé, to lament the
loss of Virginia. This character is generally devoid of interest,
and he rises to the foreground only on one occasion, when he
must be restrained from taking his own life when he realizes
his beloved is dead. More convincing is Marcus Claudius whose
qualities as a go-between are excellently defined. He enlarges
on the framework of fiction suggested by his master, filling in all
the details of the seduction and theft of the slave girl. His
oratory is persuasive to the point of even convincing friends
who have known Virginia for all her life that she might indeed
be a slave. In his resourcefulness, Marcus is not unlike the
servants of the comedies of Plautus.[12] By and large, this character is the most fully developed in the entire play and con-
tributes much to the general quality of perfection which enhances
the work which some would designate as the best tragedy in
Spanish to appear in the sixteenth century.

III   Comedia de la libertad de Roma por Mucio Cevola
      (The Comedy of the Deliverance of Rome by
      Mucius Scaevola)

Cueva's last historical play, it was performed at the Ata-
razanas in 1581. It is based on another well-known story included
by Livy in his *History of Rome*: the aftermath of the suicide of
Lucretia after being raped by Sextus Tarquinius, son of King
Tarquinius ("the Proud"). The ensuing scandal was a principal
cause for the expulsion from Rome of the Tarquinii and the
foundation of the Roman Republic. Cueva begins his drama
in medias res.

A.   *Summary*

Act I: Tarquinius is in the field when a messenger brings
word of his deposition and a warning that he will be executed
if he reenters the city. Tarquinius breaks camp and advances on

Rome despite the warning. Meanwhile, after conferring with the captain who commands the defenses of Rome, the consuls reassure the Senate that the city is safe. Reaching the walls, the deposed King calls upon the deity Quirinus for support, asking that the Romans be made to mitigate their anger and reinstate him as their king. He promises to dedicate a temple to the cult if his prayer is answered. Quirinus appears and warns him that his actions have angered Jupiter and, consequently, there is no recourse but to renounce his claim. Brutus, his captain and confidant, urges the King to disregard this warning and press an attack on the city. Tarquinius approaches the walls and—with promises of great personal gain—tries to persuade the captain of the guard to open the gates for him. Instead, the alarm is sounded, and soldiers rush to defend the city. Taunted by Brutus, Spurius Largius, the captain, throws down his glove in a challenge to the turncoat, and promises to face him in a duel as soon as the two meet in the field. The consuls repeat the edict of banishment, and spare Tarquinius' life only in deference to his past authority. The King insists that he is being unjustly punished and, in a terrible rage, he rides off to seek the aid of the Etruscan King, Porsenna, against his countrymen.

Act II: Both Porsenna and his advisor have had the same disturbing dream that prophesies the Etruscan intervention on behalf of the Roman King. Another Roman, named Sulpicio, urges Porsenna to confer with Brutus, whose arrival is announced. Although Porsenna is amazed to learn of his enemy's reversal of fortune, he receives Tarquinius in his palace and honors him at a banquet. Sulpicio advises prudence in dealing with the exiled Roman, saying that unless his request is justified, it should be rejected. Tarquinius describes his exile and the misfortunes of his family, stressing his innocence and overpowering desire for vengeance. Porsenna—more than willing to exploit the situation and turn it to his own advantage—appoints his lieutenants for the campaign. Overjoyed at the promise of revenge, Tarquinius boasts that he will be merciless against the city and will even execute the entire Senate. Sulpicio renounces any part of the enterprise which he sees as unnatural and contrary to the laws of heaven. Deaf to his advice, Porsenna erupts in a rage of indignation and orders Brutus to mutilate horribly Sulpicio who refuses to lead the attack on his countrymen. Before beginning the march, Porsenna sends the dying exile to bear testimony of his departure to the Romans.

Act III: Sulpicio reaches the city and informs the consuls of the danger, then expires. Although he had broken the terms of his banishment by returning, he is awarded a hero's burial and his honor is redeemed. As the body is consumed by the funeral pyre, word is received that the Etruscan army has attacked the Janiculum and laid siege to the city. In the calm of the next night, Brutus seeks out Spurius for the duel. The latter swears his companion to secrecy and descends by a ladder to the appointed meeting place only to find his enemy asleep. Refusing to take advantage of the helpless man, he awakens him and in the subsequent fight Brutus is mortally wounded. His body is carried off by two Furies to be deposited in Porsenna's camp.

Act IV: Because of the continuing siege, there is a serious famine and shortage of munitions. The Roman matrons urge that the consuls—who are on the verge of surrender—resist as long as there is anyone still alive to defend the city. Inspired by the gods, Mucius Scaevola volunteers to penetrate the enemy camp and assassinate Porsenna. He kills an enemy soldier who attempts to intercept him, then, dressed in the Etruscan's clothes, he enters the tent of Porsenna. The King and his paymaster are dressed identically and Mucius mistakes the paymaster for Porsenna. Stabbing him, he is at once apprehended. When ordered to identify himself, he places his arm in a burning brazier and allows the flames to consume his hand without betraying a hint of the pain he experiences. So impressed is Porsenna by the man's bravery that he spares his life. When Mucius replies that there are three hundred other Romans already in the camp who are just as determined to kill the invader, Porsenna lifts the siege and withdraws.

B. *Analysis*

As can be seen, Cueva has picked up particular motifs to develop in a concise way into a successful drama. The story of Lucretia is greatly abridged, appearing only in some thirty-five verses of narrative monologue. Likewise, Livy's emphasis on democracy and the foundation of the Republic is passed over. In order to stir the imagination of his spectators, Cueva has increased the nonhistorical elements to include dreams and omens, Furies and pagan deities, war and death, in scenes which require an elaborate stage apparatus.

The sketchy final scene involving Mucius Scaevola is, again, included only to complete the spirit of imitation and respect for his models. Far more significant for the ideological texture of the play is the effective juxtaposition of the characters and motives of the two Roman exiles, Tarquinius and Sulpicio. Cueva's purpose in writing the play was to direct his audience toward an understanding of patriotic duty. To this end, he forced a comparison of the motives of these two men and sympathy with the latter. Because of his views in regard to patriotism, Cueva devotes considerable dialogue to extol the nobility and virtue of Sulpicio.

Tarquinius begins his rôle as a problematic character. Cueva never succeeds in convincing the spectator that his banishment is the result of his own shortcomings. Throughout the first act, he is depicted as a victim of fate, a man punished for the actions of another over whom he has no control. One begins to sense that his indignation and desire for revenge are justified. Guilt by association alone seems questionable. Cueva introduces at this point in the action the moral issue about which the play will henceforth revolve—the limits of accountability conceded a wronged man bent on revenge. Tarquinius' fault will lie not in the fact that he enlisted aid in his effort to regain the throne, but rather in his choice of an enemy of the State. He fails because he renounced his obligation as a ruler to place the public safety above personal concerns.

Professor Watson's reading of the play is essentially the same. He discovers evidence of political allegory in the plot and the implied moral judgments. According to his interpretation, the situation is analagous to the tactics of Antonio, the Prior of Crato, who fled to France to enlist aid for his resistance to Philip II.[13]

CHAPTER 5

The Novelesque Plays

I   Comedia del infamador (The Comedy of the Defamer)

A. *Summary*

Act I: Leucino, a young Sevillian, attributes his amorous successes to the efficacy of wealth. Tercilo, his valet and himself
the voice of reason, counsels humility and restraint. He taunts
his master by alluding to Eliodora who resolutely rejects his
most insistent advances. Leucino ignores the rebuttal, having
already sent his servant Ortelio and an old bawd, Teodora, on a
mission of mediation on his behalf. Ortelio returns to report
the absolute failure of the visit and the severe beating of the
procuress by Eliodora's servants once the real nature of her
business was discovered. Teodora appears at Leucino's house
to collect the payment for her ill-fated undertaking whereupon
she, too, recounts the hostile reception afforded her by Eliodora.
She reassures her employer that she is willing to take similar
risks should her services be required. The setting shifts to the
banks of the Guadalquivir River as Leucino—accompanied by
Farandón, his ineffectual bodyguard—follows Eliodora into the
countryside. Although she and her servant, Felicina, attempt
to hide, they are discovered. Eliodora is predisposed to die
rather than submit to the forceful advances of her enemy.
Appealing to the river nymphs and other celestial forces, she
is saved by the intervention of Nemesis, goddess of vengeful
wrath. Despite the deity's intention of destroying him had he
harmed Eliodora, Leucino is without remorse. Ignoring the
strong warning of Nemesis, he persists with plans to possses her.

Act II: Resentful that Eliodora has eluded her powers through
Nemesis' intervention, the goddess Venus goes to the Cimmer-
ian residence of the God of Sleep who—in response to her
request—awakens his son Morpheus. This minister of sleep puts

Felicina into a trance so that Venus can assume her form and
expedite Leucino's conquest of Eliodora. Back in Seville, Farandón is sent on a predawn errand to assemble the three who can
best further his master's plans—Teodora, a second go-between
named Terecinda, and Porcero, a mutual friend favored by Ircano, the father of Eliodora. The group plots to invade the home
of Ircano when they learn of his absence. Farandón returns to
recount a humorous personal anecdote unrelated to the action.
Teodora and Terecinda perform a conjuration in which appears
a corpse with a crown, which they see as portending a felicitous
outcome.

Act III: The setting is Ircano's house. Venus, in the figure of
Felicina, discusses misogynous literature with Eliodora. Porcero
admits the bawds, who renew their plea for Leucino, claiming
that he has promised to marry Eliodora. Angered, she orders
the lot from her house, whereupon Venus reveals her identity to
Porcero and sends him to summon Leucino. When Felicina
awakens, she is unjustly accused by her mistress of complicity
in the plot to compromise her honor. With the aid of his retinue,
Leucino forces the door. Trying to defend herself, Eliodora fatally
stabs Ortelio. The arrival of the authorities coincides with that
of both Ircano and Corineo, the father of Leucino. Attempting
to account for his presence there and the cause for Ortelio's
death, Leucino resorts to deceit and defames Eliodora. He swears
that after having enjoyed intimate relations with her for more
than two years, Eliodora had rejected him for Ortelio. And that
now, enraged that the latter had revealed her secret to his
master, she had summoned them and killed Ortelio on the spot.
Eliodora's prompt denial of guilt is discredited by the perjured
corroboration of Farandón. The act ends with the imprisonment of
Eliodora and Leucino and with the two fathers each calling for
the execution of his own child for the dishonoring of the other.

Act IV: Citing legendary precedents of fathers who destroyed
their dishonored daughters, Ircano prepares to poison Eliodora.
He orders Felicina to deliver a venomous compote to her in
prison, one which miraculously turns into a bouquet of flowers
before either woman can sample it. The presiding judge enumer-
ates the many crimes of seduction committed by another prisoner
named Reicenio, whom he condemns to the stake. He then sends

a clerk to Eliodora's cell to inform her that she is to be beheaded, but the clerk is prevented from reaching the cell by two savages, ministers of the goddess Diana who then appears. Freeing Eliodora and claiming her for her legion of virginal votaries, Diana then orders Leucino to confess that he had defamed her out of anger and for no fault of her own. The savages lead Farandón to the stake, and Leucino is sentenced to be drowned in the Guadalquivir. The River God, Betis, protests the despoiling of his waters by such a vile criminal, and the play ends with the sentence being changed to that of burial alive.

B. *Analysis*

The *Comedy of the Defamer*—first performed at Seville in the patio of Doña Elvira in 1581—remains both the most celebrated and the most accessible of all Cueva's dramas. That this play should have been singled out for what now appears to be accidental distinction is due primarily to early interest in the character Leucino. Leandro Fernández de Moratín, the eighteenth-century critic and dramatist, was among the first to delve into Leucino's motivation in harassing Eliodora and his calumny of her.[1] His remarks, repeated out of context, led many historians to discover in Leucino the prototype of the Don Juan figure. The Count of Schack, Arturo Farinelli, and Gendarme de Bévotte—to cite only a few—were convinced that Leucino and Don Juan were characters from the same mold, moving from conquest to conquest, promising marriage, relying on violence and crime in a vain attempt to satiate their voracious sexual appetites.[2]

More recently, Francisco A. de Icaza's reading has been reiterated, for the most part, by Professors Joseph E. Gillet and Ángel Valbuena Prat.[3] All three attempt to rectify the widespread misconceptions, insisting that Leucino's monomania is really the vindication of the power of wealth. They conclude, and rightly so, that Leucino is essentially unlike Tirso de Molina's seventeenth-century dramatization of the *Burlador de Sevilla* (*The Seducer of Seville*). Professor J. P. Wickersham Crawford's assertion that the work is a rudimentary example of what would later be called the "Cape and Sword" play only confuses the issue.[4]

As the plot summary indicates, the play lacks the essential feature of the Don Juan legend which once constituted the major interest of Tirso's play, namely, the invitation of a corpse to dinner. One may reasonably conclude that Cueva's play—for which no single literary source has been postulated—as well as Tirso's, derives from diverse traditions which may well include legend.[5]

Of particular importance for the action of the play is the motif of the false accusation of the chaste woman, which has many historical and literary antecedents. Eliodora's stoic refusal to bend to Leucino's indecent demands and her preference of death to dishonor both suggest the legend of Lucretia and Sextus Tarquinius. A Roman matron who killed herself after being raped, Lucretia became synonymous with all the sentiments of moral virtue invoked by the memory of her justifiable self-martyrdom. Both Dante and St. Augustine—in imitation of other writers who extol her—held a favorable view of her suicide.

Cueva's treatment of the conflict suggests possible hagiographic influences. In the thirteenth century, Alfonso X, King of Castile—in the 186th of his collection of miracles of the Virgin—alludes to the case of a virtuous wife who is falsely accused of adultery by her jealous mother-in-law. The treacherous woman sends a Negro into the bedchamber, then calls the husband to witness the offense. The Virgin intervenes to save the wife who has been sentenced to the stake. Leucino's temptation of Eliodora also bears resemblances to the story of the Sts. Cyprian and Justina, whose lives were later dramatized by Spain's greatest theologian-dramatist, Pedro Calderón de la Barca. Saintly legend, indeed, is suggested by the transformation of the poisonous preserves into flowers.

Finally, it is worth noting in this discussion of influences that the false accusation was a favorite recourse of writers who drew extensively on the stock situation of the Italian *novelle*, or short stories. Both Juan de Timoneda and Alonso de la Vega, dramatists of the mid-sixteenth century, had glossed the story of the love of Don Giovanni of Mendoza for the Duchess of Savoya and the miracle that befalls them. Their source is the complicated second part of Matteo Bandello's *Novella XLIV*. Lope de Vega would later revitalize the theme in several of his early dramas, reversing the male and female rôles as he does, for example, in *Carlos el perseguido* (*The Harassment of Charles*).

The drama is most plausibly interpreted as a mythological play in which Cueva combined multiple dramatic traditions. One, the appearance and intervention of gods and goddesses in the affairs of mortals brings reminiscences of the medieval debates and the dramatic eclogues of Juan del Encina and his imitators. In these compositions, Venus and Cupid punish men and women who, as does Eliodora, repudiate their authority to govern love. An interesting feature of the play is the pride and competition between the three goddesses Nemesis, Venus, and Diana as each tries to gain the upper hand. José Caso González observes, in his edition of the play (Salamanca: Ediciones Anaya, 1965), that the inclusion of characters from classical mythology goes beyond the mere intent to resolve the action and that Nemesis, "as a personification of the moral indignation felt when natural harmony is disturbed, might signify the victory of chastity over Leucino's intent to rape" (p. 24).

The most salient feature of the play is the motif of the go-between incorporated in the portrayal of Teodora and Terecinda. While it is not in itself proof of Cueva's familiarity with the *Celestina* attributed to Fernando de Rojas, his inclusion of the type assures him of a place in the long tradition that includes the characters Fulgencia and Eritea of Juan del Encina's *Eclogue of Plácida and Vitoriano* (1513) and culminates with such ones as Marcela in Lope de Vega's *La bella malmaridada* (*The Beautiful Adulteress*), ca. 1588.

These two bawds are pale shadows of Spain's infamous Celestina of some eighty-odd years before.[6] Indeed, the only common trait which they share is an expertise in magic and sorcery. We read that Terecinda can slip out of her house through a trap-door and appear on the street faster than fire can rise to the heavenly region of flame. The incantations and augury at the end of the second act suggest a possible influence of Virgil and Seneca, and may even be modeled on a similar invocation by Celestina.

Although Cueva is not usually distinguished by the creation of memorable character types, the rôle of Farandón is an exception. This braggart servant's illusions of militant bravado can be traced to his prototype, a stock character of the Italian *commedia dell'arte*.[7] Farandón's descriptive monologue in which he drunkenly challenges all comers outside his master's house is the most humorous scene of the play.

The most recent development in criticism of this important play is A. I. Watson's discovery of a substratum of political allegory.[8] He contends that the similarity between this work and another—*El viejo enamorado* (*The Old Man in Love*)—is "best explained in terms of a common political allegory" (p. 181). Professor Watson correctly singles out the importance of the first act in which Cueva stresses Leucino's vision of money as a panacea. Watson's thesis is, in essence, that Leucino is a literary counterpart of Philip II, and the hostile young women who fail to respond to his offers of money "may well symbolise those countries and provinces which were hostile to Philip, with Eliodora as the personification of Portugal" (p. 185). Furthermore, this critic finds: "On the political plane Teodora corresponds with any of the numerous envoys, official and unofficial, whom Philip sent to plead his case before Cardinal Henry and the Lisbon Chamber, whose members reacted almost as harshly to Philip's overtures as Eliodora does to those of Leucino" (pp. 186-87). This fascinating interpretation imparts a new and deeper significance to Teodora's vision of the death's-head and crown: "As Leucino chased the crown about the stage some of the more politically-minded members of Cueva's audience might perhaps have related what they saw to the many anxieties and frustrations undergone by their King in his bid for the crown of Portugal" (p. 193).

II Comedia del viejo enamorado (The Comedy of the Old Man in Love)

A. *Summary*

Act I: The aged Liboso learns that his friend and mediator, Versilo, has not been able to persuade Festilo to grant the hand of his daughter Olimpia in marriage because she is already promised to Arcelo. Before Festilo arrives to discuss the matter, Liboso decides to order his servant Barandulo to swear that Arcelo is already married. Versilo detains Festilo long enough

for Liboso to instruct Barandulo as to his future rôle. Festilo is
appalled at the revelation. Preferring to verify the facts himself,
he concedes that if it can be established that Arcelo is, in fact,
already married, he will gladly give his daughter to the octogenarian. Barandulo produces his bawdy mistress, Doña Alba
de Miranda, who plays the rôle of the wronged wife. Despite
Arcelo's indignant protests of innocence, the masquerade convinces Festilo, who then offers Olimpia to Liboso. The latter
sends his servant to challenge Arcelo to a duel before the deceit
is discovered. Unexpectedly, three supernatural figures—the
Fury Lissa, Envy, and Discord—align themselves against Liboso.
Disguised as men, they infiltrate his household to incite him to
attack Arcelo.

Act II: Festilo is shocked to learn that his daughter rejects the
newly-found suitor. Steadfast in her love for Arcelo, she prefers
suicide to renunciation. Calling on Love to restore his lost
honor, Arcelo is overheard weeping by Olimpia, who is soon convinced of his sincerity. Meanwhile, Barandulo—spying the pair
—admits to himself that his public bravura masks a coward's
heart. Arcelo is annoyed by his conciliatory air and dalliance,
but accepts the challenge to meet Liboso on the dueling field.
While Olimpia tries to dissuade her lover from risking his life,
Liboso nervously awaits the return of the braggart servant.
Barandulo reports that Arcelo is raging, and Liboso prudently
decides that, at his age, he is no match for a young rival. In
desperation Liboso orders that his friend, the magician Rogerio,
be summoned to deal with Arcelo. The necromancer offers two
alternatives—an infernal apparition to startle Arcelo and make
him more vulnerable to the other's sword, or the Furies to spirit
him away to a mountain prison. The disguised supernatural
beings attempt to coerce Liboso to select the first choice, but
the magician forces them to resume their true forms, then orders
the Fury Lissa and her sisters to abduct Arcelo at the moment
of confrontation.

Act III: Arcelo confidently departs to meet his adversary,
disregarding Olimpia's entreaties that he remain with her. At
first determined to accompany him, she agrees to send her page
to protect her lover. Liboso arrives first and Rogerio tells him
how to proceed if the spell is to work. As planned, the Furies

carry Arcelo through the air before the duel begins. The frightened page flees to raise the alarm. Liboso's joy at success is eclipsed by Rogerio's description of adverse omens which portend punishment for the conspirators. Olimpia comes seeking news of the outcome and, seeing the two together, realizes the cause of her misfortune and plots to turn each against the other. Pretending to correspond to his love, she orders Liboso to kill his friend. Meanwhile, smitten with love for Olimpia, Rogerio stalks the old man. In the ensuing encounter, Liboso stabs the magician repeatedly, only to be struck down by Olimpia. About to take her own life, the virgin is restrained by the personification of Reason, who offers to guide her to her lover's prison in the nearby mountain. As Olimpia departs—having been told the magic rite required for Arcelo's freedom—a search party discovers the bodies of the two schemers which are thrown into the waters of the Guadalquivir.

Act IV: In pastoral guise, the Fury Lissa guards Arcelo in his cavernous cell. At dawn the searchers arrive, but—misdirected by the "shepherd"—they fall and suffer grave injuries. The god Hymen, also dressed as a shepherd, waits to guide Olimpia safely over the treacherous paths to the cave entrance. Festilo and his men are amazed to encounter her there where they have unsuccessfully tried to punish Lissa for her betrayal of them. With the aid of Hymen, Lissa is subdued long enough for Olimpia to perform the magic which opens the cave door. Disclosing his true identity, Hymen enters and brings Arcelo out. The play concludes with the return of Lissa to the underworld and the joyous reunion of the lovers.

B. *Analysis*

Cueva combines in this violent comedy the *senex-virgo* motif of Roman comedy with that of the pretended marriage. The latter was a frequently employed device of the *commedia dell'-arte,* and was particularly popular with such later French playwrights as Molière and Scarron. Although this is essentially a mythological play, Crawford finds fault with the later acts and the intervention of the Furies (p. 169). Actually, Cueva's expansion of Lissa's rôle is in keeping with his humanistic insistence

on truth and verisimilitude. He says of her in the prose summary of the action that she is "a Fury named Lissa, and not a
kind of fish as some have said in ignorance of the name; she was
created by Juno to punish Hercules as she is portrayed by Euripides in his *Hercules Enraged.*" The necromancy motif and the
intervention of the magician to promote an ill-fated marriage
would soon be exploited by Lope de Vega in one of his earliest
novelesque plays, *El ganso de oro* (*The Golden Goose*).

Cueva's portrayal of Barandulo is the most effective feature
of the entire work. Harking back to the Plautine *miles gloriosus,*
he also shares common features with Centurio of the *Celestina*:
his inherent cowardice concealed by empty boasts of violent
propensities, his association with disreputable types, and his
slightly off-color brand of humor. Even the ingenuity of his
concubine echoes reminiscences of Rojas' work. Clearly, the play
is labeled a comedy precisely because of the lowly backgrounds
of the characters portrayed.

This work has awakened little critical interest. Watson, arguing for contemporary historical parallels in the action, has hit
upon a rather interesting point: "Any interpretation of *El viejo
enamorado* which is not based on the existence of a political
allegory at its heart will have to explain why it is that, although
Liboso is an octogenarian, on no occasion does Olimpia object
to marrying him on the grounds of his advanced age. Her hatred
towards him is as absolute and unexplained as her love for
Arcelo" (p. 179). Professor Watson goes on to posit that in
Cueva's mind Olimpia was the counterpart of Portugal and
Liboso of Philip II. He further identifies Barandulo with "the
aggressive aspect of the pretender's policy" and Rogerio with
"the Fox of Machiavellian statecraft" (p. 180).

III   Comedia del degollado (The Comedy of the Beheaded Man)

A. *Summary*

Act I: Arnaldo, captain of a Spanish galleon, discusses with
his servant the exceptional bravery of the Moor Chichivali, taken
prisoner in a naval encounter. The servant criticizes his master
for laxness in freeing the man on the condition that he later

provide ransom. Leaving the question aside, Arnaldo turns to
the preparations for a banquet at which he plans to honor his
beloved, Celia, and some of her friends. Chichivali and another
Moor, Palique, sail to Arnaldo's island stronghold to pay the
ransom. Arriving, the former confesses that although he is
free, his heart has been captured by Celia whom he now hopes
to abduct. Disguised as a Christian, Palique goes out to search
for her. She—misunderstanding the purpose of the banquet—
dresses as a man in order to spy on her lover during the party.
Arnaldo broods over her absence from his table when the cry
is raised that Moors are attacking the city. Chichivali, carrying
a flag of truce, approaches Arnaldo with the ransom. The Christian is unable to persuade him to remain as a guest for a few
days. A servant reports that Celia has been taken prisoner by the
Moors and that they have set sail for their land. Arnaldo prepares to go to her rescue, but is taken prisoner by Palique who
had remained behind in search of captives.

Act II: The Moorish captains present their captives to the
aging King, who has just abdicated in favor of his young son.
When Chichivali recognizes Arnaldo, he asks the King to free
him in order to avoid a conflict over Celia. Claiming that Celia
is his brother, Arnaldo pleads for her release also. Arnaldo is
permitted to speak with her and urges Celia to continue the
masquerade. Meanwhile Chichivali informs the Prince of Celia's
true identity. The young monarch is indignant at the betrayal
of Arnaldo's friendship and orders Chichivali from his sight. He
himself begins to feel a growing lust for Celia, aroused by the
description of her by the captain. Speaking with Arnaldo, he
learns that "Celio" is an accomplished musician, and he asks for
a performance.

Act III: After Celia sings, the Prince openly declares his love.
The two engage in ambiguous verbal play based on her male
disguise. She finally leaves the Prince sleeping, only to be
pursued by Chichivali. When the latter forces himself on her,
Arnaldo intervenes, and the Moor is killed. Arnaldo is imprisoned,
and Celia confesses to the Prince, who rejects her culpability.

Act IV: The Prince laments his unrequited love, followed by
Palique's praise of Arnaldo's virtue in the face of the King's
death sentence. Celia asks the Prince to spare her lover, and he

agrees on the condition that she must accede to his wishes. He
then arranges with the jailer to substitute another condemned
man for Arnaldo. The Spaniard is brought before his benefactor
who hides him in his own quarters. The young Prince is unsure
how to proceed. Thinking the dead man she has seen is Arnaldo,
Celia accuses the Prince of failing to keep his word. Arnaldo
is summoned forth only after Celia reiterates her promise to
the Prince. Overcome by sympathy for the constant lovers, the
Prince frees them both in a display of selfless compassion.

B. *Analysis*

In this play Cueva returns to the theme of the sentimental
Moor, which he treats in his plays for the first time in the history
of the Spanish drama. The traditional enemy is portrayed as the
possessor of the attributes most revered by Christendom. The
opening dialogue establishes a striking similarity to the *Historia
de Abindarráez y Jarifa,* an anonymous tale included in Villegas'
Inventario (1565). Virtue is the foundation stone of both works.
Cueva, as did his predecessor, clearly defines virtue as the highest attribute inherent in gentlemen of both races. His dramatic
definition traces the word to the etymological origins: Latin *vir,*
man, i.e., the quality of being a man. Strength and courage are,
of course, synonymous with manliness, but more important—as
the Prince's conduct illustrates—the supreme test is the ability
to dominate one's passions and reward the virtue of another.
The effectiveness of the play derives from the unexpected moral
collapse of Chichivali—whose initial virtue is only a veneer—
and the tardy introduction of the Prince. His victory over his
desire for Celia more than compensates for the abuses perpe-
trated by his countryman.

The moral problem is well resolved in the concluding scene.
Arnaldo's virtue requires that he honor the pledge made by
Celia to her suitor, even at the cost of his own happiness.
Cueva's rule that magnanimity must correspond to magnanimity
permits the satisfactory ending. A similar moral dilemma is the
basis for the fourth tale in Boccaccio's *Questioni d'amore* (*Love
Disputes*), and was also treated in several works by Giraldi
Cinthio.[10] Lope de Vega would soon turn to the theme of Moor-

ish captivity and midnight raids in his youthful play *El grao de Valencia* (*The Valencia Dockyard*). Professor Crawford points out that the play "has interesting points of similarity with Whetstone's *Historye of Promos and Cassandra* and with Shakespeare's *Measure for Measure*" (p. 169).

IV Comedia del tutor (The Comedy of the Guardian)

A. *Summary*

Act I: The young student Otavio's love soliloquy is cut short by his servant, Licio, who reports the completion of a portrait of Aurelia which had been commissioned on the eve of his departure for Salamanca. When he goes for the portrait, Licio tells his old guardian, Dorildo, that he has gone to purchase textbooks. Skeptical, Dorildo sends the servant to find his master who must leave Seville for the university at once. Licio realizes that Dorildo's concern for his ward is merely a subterfuge since the old man also loves Aurelia. Licio complains to her of Dorildo's specious display of decorum when his illicit affairs have made him the mockery of the city. Otavio assures his beloved that absence will not diminish his love, but the guardian interrupts the pledges of constancy to hasten Otavio's departure. Once he has left, Dorildo offers to console Aurelia who spurns his advances.

Act II: At the university, Otavio's portrait of Aurelia incites the lust of his friend Leotacio. Entrusting his home to the Sevillian, he prepares to seek her out under the pretext of courting another lady. His servant, Astropo, tries in vain to dissuade him. Meanwhile, Aurelia resists the importunate advances of Dorildo for many months. Licio brings letters from Salamanca, and reports that Otavio is leading an exemplary scholar's life. Dorildo confesses to him his passion for Aurelia and asks his assistance in winning her. Though he at first refuses, Licio finally consents. Accepting gifts and money, Licio suggests that he will use them to bribe Aurelia to accede to the old man's desires. Leotacio likewise seeks Licio's mediation on his behalf. Agreeing again to promote this cause, Licio then jokes with Aurelia about the gullibility of her suitors. She gives permission for

Licio to expose both to public ridicule as punishment for their betrayal of Otavio.

Act III: Determined to deceive both Dorildo and Leotacio simultaneously, Licio arranges for the latter to be lodged in the guardian's house. Ten day later, Licio—dressed as a torch-carrying devil—enters Leotacio's room. Both the student and his servant are so badly frightened that they awaken their host who makes light of their fear. Refusing to reenter the room, Astropo deserts his master and returns to Salamanca.

Act IV: Astropo delivers to Otavio a letter from Licio informing him of the deception of his friends and urging his immediate return. Eleven days later, he discovers Licio in the streets and is hidden away in Aurelia's home until vengeance can be taken. Licio informs both suitors that Aurelia has consented to a late-night assignation but that each must dress in a showy fashion to impress her. First Licio leads Dorildo—resplendently foolish in his youthful dress—to a darkened street corner. While waiting for Aurelia, he is embarrassed by the authorities who require him to reveal his identity. Next Licio takes Leotacio to the same spot. Then, disguised as women, Otavio and Licio join the unsuspecting suitors who chat with them. Aurelia then appears and unveils each "lady," whereupon Dorildo and the guardian suffer extreme mortification.

B. *Analysis*

The *Comedy of the Guardian*—performed at the Huerta of Doña Elvira in 1579—is the least pretentious of Cueva's plays. That he considered it more of an expanded farce than anything else is indicated in one of Licio's many confidential asides to the audience: "Have you ever seen such an amusing farce?/ Did Saldaña ever once in his life/ come up with a more intricate plot/ as good as he was at conceiving them?" Licio's puns, raucous *joie de vivre*, and scatological allusions contribute much to the humorous tone of the play. Crawford likens him to "a resourceful Sempronio" (p. 168). Astropo provides as much comedy in his rôle of braggart servant torn between a manly façade and the almost feminine logic upon which he relies to avoid any confrontation.

The play is clearly an adaptation of Roman comedy of the type that was most successful in the hands of Torres Naharro and, to a lesser degree, in those of Rueda and Timoneda. Writing of the *dramatis personae,* Morby economically summarizes Cueva's debt to Roman models: "...the young man, often a student who cannot solve his problems himself; the servants, often real conductors of the intrigue; the comic old man (either a niggardly father or an enamoured gallant); the braggart, and the hetaera, either vicious or a good influence."[11]

V   Comedia de la constancia de Arcelina
(The Comedy of Arcelina's Constancy)

A.   Summary

Act I: Fulcino complains to his servant that Arcelina rejects his love for that of Menalcio. Gelcino reproves his master's homicidal urges. Arcelina warns her sister, Crisea, to cease her rivalry for Menalcio, but is told that this is impossible. Crisea proposes that the question be left to chance, and the two sisters prepare to draw lots. Gelcino warns the ladies that Fulcino plots to harm them. Arcelina sends him back with the admonition that love is never deterred by fear. Menalcio soliloquizes on his inability to choose between the two sisters. When Arcelina objects to the procedure for drawing the lots, Crisea suggests that Menalcio be asked to do it. The drawing is indecisive because blank lots appear each time. Menalcio refuses to favor either lady when each offers an article of clothing for a second drawing. Blaming Crisea for Menalcio's hasty departure, Arcelina murders her sister, then flees into the countryside. Menalcio is found beside the body by the authorities. Perjuring himself, Fulcino testifies that he had witnessed Menalcio murder the girl, whereupon his rival is jailed.

Act II: Fulcino consults the necromancer Orbante, who conjures up a multitude of infernal shades—the Fury Tisiphone, and the spirits of Zoroaster, Achilles, Isis, Aegisthus and Dido. From them Fulcino learns that he is destined to die because of a mistaken identity. Arcelina's hiding place in the nearby mountain is also revealed.

Act III: The shepherd Pastulcio searches for Olimpio, another shepherd, who has stolen his wife. Fearful of discovery, Arcelina hides from him, but the shepherd attacks thinking she is his enemy. She saves herself pretending to be Pallas, patroness of the shepherds. The contrite rustic agrees to redeem himself in her eyes by bringing to her news from the village. Fulcino encounters Olimpio and—after inquiring in vain after Arcelina—accepts his shepherd's clothing to renew the search. Mistaken for their owner, Fulcino is accidentally killed by Pastulcio as he sets out for the village. Arcelina's father, Arcedio, is consoled by his friend, Laercio. Pastulcio overhears their conversation, then reports to "Pallas" that Menalcio has been sentenced to die for her crime. She resolves to surrender in order that he be saved.

Act IV: Although the townsmen appeal to the Governor to postpone execution, Menalcio is taken to the gallows as Arcelina reaches the site. She stops the executioner and—summoning the authorities—confesses her guilt. The Governor pretends to consult Arcedio concerning a different case and extracts from him a pardon for Arcelina.

B. *Analysis*

Because of the seemingly unjustifiable exculpation of the murderess and the failure to punish Pastulcio, this work, especially, has disturbed the critics.[12] Crawford, calling it "an extravagant play" (p. 168), goes on to object in the strongest of terms: "One ridiculous situation follows another until an absurd *dénouement* is reached which violates every law of probability" (pp. 168-69). Watson—suspicious of Crawford's superficial reading—cautions against hasty judgments: "Cueva was later to write novelesque plays whose extraordinary plots would appear to be best explained by his desire to parallel contemporary political events and it is possible that he was experimenting with something similar when he wrote this play" (p. 116). He admits, however, that such a correlation is not easily perceived.

The most satisfactory interpretation to date is that of John W. Battle who reads the play as a warning against passionate love and the elucidation of the fallibility of justice. Professor Battle further argues that in this play Cueva reveals the pattern of sin-repentance-forgiveness which is central to his Christian world view.[13] Morby is doubtless correct in tracing Cueva's curious combination of motifs to the first novel of the Introduction to Giraldi Cinthio's collection.[14]

VI   Comedia *and* Tragedia del príncipe tirano
(The Comedy *and the* Tragedy of the Tyrant Prince)

These two dramas with the same title—one a comedy and the other a tragedy—form one long play, the second being a sequel to the first. They were, in all probability, performed at the same time—in the Huerta of Doña Elvira in 1580. Cueva earns for himself with these plays the distinction of being the first Spanish playwright to compose a two-part drama.

A.   *Summary of the* Comedy

Act I: King Agelao of Colchis discusses with the Prince the proposed marriage of Princess Royal Eliodora to the King of Lydia—contracted to ensure peace between the two kingdoms. He explains to his young son that he will only assume the throne in the event that Lido and Eliodora have no issue, but in compensation grants Licimaco dominion over the great city of Phasis. Outwardly appearing to accept the treaty, Licimaco soon plots to undermine the agreement. He is urged by the grandee Tracildoro and the Fury Alecto—masquerading as his nurse Merope—to murder his sister. He wastes no time in carrying out the plan to ambush her and bury the body in the garden. The three Fates are seen spinning the thread of life, measuring it and finally cutting it. Once the deed is done, Licimaco executes his friend to ensure secrecy. When his sister's absence is noticed, the Prince allows Agelao's wrath to fall on Merope and her husband, Gracildo, who are bound over for torture.

Act II: The spirits of Eliodora and Tracildoro harass the Prince and the King, demanding proper burial. The ghost of the girl warns Agelao to punish the one closest to him, but Licimaco convinces his father that the allusion must be to the nurse and her husband whom Agelao promptly condemns to death. The grandee Cratilo conjures up the ghosts who reveal the

Prince's guilt in time to prevent the execution. Agelao orders his son imprisoned until he can select a punishment so harsh that he will be made an example of. He is placed under the guard of Gracildo.

Act III: Agelao names judges to try Licimaco. Though he is condemned to death, the grandees argue that such action would be detrimental to the kingdom and urge his exoneration. The Prince asks his jailer to free him, and out of fear Gracildo reveals a tunnel that he had dug while in the cell. He then asks to be relieved of his duties so that he will not have to watch the execution of the child he had reared.

Act IV: The Prince flees his cell and takes refuge in the home of the grandee Beraldo. Meanwhile, other grandees press their demand that Agelao commute the sentence of public mutilation which he has, himself, ordered. News of the escape is brought, and Agelao is furious at the negligence of the new jailer. Beraldo intercedes on the Prince's behalf and, against his better judgment, the King acquiesces to popular demand and pardons his son. The grandees swear allegiance to their Prince as the play ends.

B. *Summary of the* Tragedy

Act I: Licimaco voices his desire to rule the world. When Agelao speaks of abdication, the Prince at first pretends to have no interest in ruling while his father is alive. Three men and a girl request an audience at which Agelao must decide which suitor the father will favor with his daughter's hand in marriage. He blindfolds the girl who—following her natural inclinations—selects the man whom she really loves. As the Council assembles for the abdication ceremony, it is learned that the commoners oppose the accession of the Prince. Thunder and earth tremors herald the entrance of a mute carrying a book, which he tears in two, and a sickle, with which he cuts his own throat. Licimaco reassures his father that the bizarre occurrence portends no misfortune.

Act II: The next morning, the grandees begin to doubt the wisdom of their support of Licimaco when they learn of his atrocious punishment of his servants for a minor offense. Helpless to deter his mad and cruel excesses, they leave for the coronation ceremonies. Just as the grandees kneel to accept the new monarch, the investiture is interrupted by the personification of the Kingdom with his chest pierced by a sword. Although he interprets the symbolism of the mute's pantomime, he concludes that tyranny will be replaced by peace.

Act III: Licimaco begins his rule by razing the temple and destroying the archives which contain the privileges of the people. He orders Teodosia, the wife of his cousin Calcedio, to leave her husband and become his mistress. When Ericipo asks his assistance in making peace between two quarreling friends, Licimaco orders him to surrender his daughter for his pleasure. Learning that Gracildo and Cratilo disapprove of his conduct, the Prince has them bound and thrown from a tower. The aggrieved citizenry appeals to Agelao to deliver them from the tyrant, but he is ineffective. Licimaco's murders include that of his nurse and her grandchild. Finally, in mockery of Ericipo's request, Licimaco binds the left hands of the quarrelers and orders them to fight to the death for his amusement during dinner. Agelao arrives in time to free them, and the Prince threatens to have him hanged should he interfere again.

Act IV: Licimaco has Calcedio and Ericipo brought before him and buried chest-deep in the ground beside his banquet table. Leaving them to be torn to pieces by ferocious dogs, he departs intending to ravish their women. Before this can happen, Teodosia and Doriclea are able to murder the tyrant. Agelao frees the buried men, pardons the homicide of his son, and orders the body cast into the fields.

C. *Analysis*

Although no precise models for these plays are known, it is clear that Cueva comes closest in them to imitating Senecan horror than in any other works. His choice of setting may have been suggested by Herodotus who gives a vague description of Colchis, mentions Phasis, and refers to an alliance with the kingdom of Lydia.[15]

These two plays are rich in thematic and ideological content. Icaza—failing to consider them as mutually dependent—concluded that Cueva condones the murder of Eliodora because the Prince is not punished at the end of the *Comedy*. Watson—whose interpretation is eminently successful—writes that Cueva "neither defends immorality in his characters nor does he stand aside and adopt an amoral attitude" (p. 149). This critic's argument for political allegory in the two plays is summarized as follows: "Cueva was suggesting to the audience that if [Cardinal] Henry succumbed to the wishes of the Portuguese nobility for purely expediential reasons and handed over his kingdom to Spain without the consent of the third estate, then Portugal might suffer a similar fate to Colchis and fall into the hands of a tyrant" (p. 205).

It should be noted that these two plays are of exceptional interest also because of their thematic proximity to Spain's greatest theological drama—*La vida es sueño* (*Life is an Illusion*)—composed by Calderón de la Barca nearly half a century later. The characters of Licimaco and Segismundo—his Calderonian counterpart—bear a striking similarity. Cueva's scene—in the first act of the *Comedy*—in which the Fates argue the possibility of postponing Eliodora's death is especially significant in the light of the theological overtones of the later work. Licimaco's decision to kill Tracildoro is paralleled by Segismundo's realization that once the revolution to place him on the throne has succeeded, there is no need for the treasonous soldier who freed him.

CHAPTER 6

The Lyric Poetry

D URING the course of his life—and especially in his youth—
Juan de la Cueva composed verses in a great many modes.
Some, little more than literary exercises, are very inconsequen-
tial. Others, conceived with true lyric intuition, are highly
successful. Most attest Cueva's lifelong debt to the rich sources
of classical inspiration whose imprint is deep indeed. In the
extension and variety of his poetry, he is similar to the humanist
writers of the Italian Renaissance. Regrettably, this large segment of his writings is very inaccessible. As has been noted
already, only a portion was ever published—in the volume
entitled *Obras de Juan de la Cueva, dedicadas al ilustrísimo
señor don Juan Téllez Girón* . . . (*The Works of Juan de la Cueva,
Dedicated to the Most Illustrious Gentleman, Don Juan Téllez
Girón* . . .). Only a few copies of this edition are known to have
survived, and it was never reprinted. Well over half of the poems
by Cueva exist only in manuscript versions, none of which has
been published in its entirety. For this reason, very few hispanists have any idea just what the nature of Cueva's poetry really
is. In the interest of clarifying this facet of the complete opus,
there follows a summary of the poet's total production in this
vein, including both published and manuscript works.

Twenty-five elegies (*elegías*), twelve of which appear in the
Works. A formal poem, the genre once was reserved exclusively
for funeral eulogy. By Cueva's day, the elegy tended to be of
two basic types. In the most common, often referred to as heroic,
the poet laments the loss of a great public figure or a national
disaster. Exceptional among the latter is Herrera's poem, "On
the Loss of King Sebastian," in which he recalls the Portuguese
defeat at the Battle of Alcazar-Kebir. A second variety, more
intimate and personal, alludes to individual rather than collective sorrow. Cueva's elegies, all in tercets, belong to this category.

101

Unrequited love and despair at the beloved's cruelty constitute the essence of these poems.

Twenty-one *canciones*—the Spanish equivalent of the Italian *canzone*—which is not to be confused with the anonymous, popular song, native to the Spanish lyric tradition. Again love is the theme of these compositions, which are modeled on those of Petrarch. As a rule, Cueva is consistent in adherence to the structural requirements of the genre—development of a single idea, each strophe being devoted to one aspect of the unifying concept.

Two hundred sixty-six sonnets, more than half unpublished. These poems cover a wider variety of subjects than some of the other genres. Many are, of course, amatory and describe Cueva's love for "Felicia." A great many honor the literati of Seville: Baltasar del Alcázar, Herrera, Mal Lara, Francisco de Medina, etc. Some are moral as, for example, the sonnets on penitence and fortitude. Of considerable interest are those which describe contemporary celebrations or disasters as, for example, the flooding of the Guadalquivir in December of 1604. Cueva's poetic intuition reaches a culmination in the occasional pieces, often burlesque, which indicate his growing interest in the sonnet as an anti-genre. Originally the sonnet was conceived for the purpose of ennobling or enhancing reality almost beyond the point of recognition. In the post-Renaissance years the form suffered exceptional thematic debasement as poets focused their attention on the grotesque and ignoble aspects of human experience.

Many of Cueva's sonnets place him one step farther along the path to the complete perversion of the genre which would permit Baroque poets to take outrageous liberties with the sonnet and describe, for instance, a man deformed by an enormous nose, or a lady bitten on the bosom by a flea. Among the most successful of this type are Cueva's sonnets about the cure for Venus' morning sickness and his mockery of a lady who is indignant that she should have been caught spinning wool. Cueva seems to have delighted in making sport of those who are unduly superstitious, since several sonnets are dedicated to the subject. In one he ridicules a man who had been frightened by the crowing of a cock and the barking of a dog at dusk. Urging the fellow to take heart, Cueva admits mockingly, "I have been tortured by a thousand cowbells,/ and just yesterday a monkey made faces at me/ but I laugh at ill-luck."[1]

Two long mythological fables: "Llanto de Venus en la muerte de Adonis" ("Venus' Lament for the Dead Adonis") and the burlesque "Amores de Marte y Venus" ("Loves of Mars and Venus"). The first was included in the *Works*, and the second is found in three manuscripts.[2] Both are in octaves, though the "Lament" is only half as long as the "Loves." Cueva expanded the former in his manuscript, "The Second Part of the Works . . . ," where it is increased by forty-two octaves, bringing the total number of verses very near that of the other fable. The expanded version has been edited by Paul Verdevoye.[3]

In both poems Cueva displays his diligence as a craftsman, his intellectual concentration, and sedulous attention to detail. "Venus' Lament" contains a good deal more plot material than the title indicates. It encompasses the entire myth and includes several details not supplied by Ovid's *Metamorphoses*: Omens portending tragedy precede the hunt which Cueva describes with sharp realism. Venus' grief is protracted throughout seven octaves, and it is so emotive that it is shared by many other deities who come to console her. Even infernal gods appear to witness the solemnity of the burial ceremonies.

Of particular interest is Cueva's treatment of fate and free will. When Venus demands of Jupiter the reason why he did not prevent the tragedy, the god replies that even his power is limited: "Invincible Fate is to blame/ for as long as man lives,/ destiny imposes irrevocable limits/ so that no god whatsoever/ can add or take away a single moment of life." It should be noted that Cueva and his generation employed mythology systematically not for exemplary ends, but simply to embellish their works with classical ornamentation. In their attitudes toward pagan mythology, they did not perceive a conflict between Catholicism and the Classics. Christian piety was unshaken by the revival of pagan legends precisely because of the great care taken centuries before by St. Thomas Aquinas in reconciling neoclassical theory with Catholic dogma.[4] As would be expected, Cueva's use of mythology here and elsewhere is strictly an external, formal element of his art.

Two madrigals—short lyric poems based on the medieval Italian model by the same name. A simple amatory subject is the most common. Belonging to the genre of the epigram, this verse form is generally a free combination of seven and eleven syllable lines. Cueva's own countryman from Seville, Gutierre de Cetina (1520-1557), was largely responsible for the vogue of the form in Spain. The subject of both of Cueva's madrigals is unrequited love. In the first, "I endure the disdain and the wrath," he typically insists on the anonymity of the beloved. The second, "Lovely eyes, cease your cruelty," is notable for the effective use of a favorite figure of speech, a form of repetition termed anadiplosis.

Mention should also be made of Cueva's lone attempt at the *sextina*. Somewhat less common in Spanish than the other Italianate strophes, this form was also tried by Cetina. Consisting of six hendecasyllabic verses, it was employed for a variety of themes. Cueva's poem, "Apollo appears with the first rays of dawn," is a conventional declaration of unrequited love pronounced by the despondent poet who weeps by the banks of the Betis.

Seven eclogues—idealized bucolic poems conceived in the Virgilian spirit. The pastoral guise is, typically, only a pretense, the shepherds betraying their courtly sensitivities and reflecting on the very real concerns of the day. Cueva prefers a strophic variety for his eclogues, employing octaves, tercets, and *canciones* which he sometimes alternates in a single poem. Although it is not always possible to identify them, the interlocutors of his eclogues have real-life counterparts, and the pastoral anecdotes are actually thinly-veiled equivalents of contemporary happenings of Seville. For example, Fernando de Herrera appears as the shepherd Iolas in the fourth eclogue which Cueva rather daringly dedicated to Álvaro de Portugal, his lover's husband.

Perhaps the most puzzling is the first eclogue. Cueva teasingly mentions in one manuscript version that the names of the shepherds, Alcyone and Caustino, are allegorically significant. In the dedicatory verses—to Antonio Manrique, commander of the convoy with which Cueva returned from Mexico—the poet alludes to "these difficult times" and to his "secret fear." Speaking conventionally, he promises to dedicate more works to Manrique once he is free from the travails which oppress him. Wulff suspects that Alcyone is Cueva himself.[5] If he is right, this eclogue could provide further clues as to the author's amatory involvements on the eve of his return to Spain.

The poem treats a rather standard lovers' triangle: Caustino is loved by the shepherdess Cynthia, but his friend Alcyone falls in love with her. Cueva introduces a rival in the fourth shepherd, Anfriso, whose disruptive influence causes unnatural changes in Alcyone. Cueva's poetic world is here remarkably similar to the one created by Garcilaso in his famous first eclogue: Nature provides a pattern of order and harmony which should reign in the universe. It is Nature's law that love should answer love. By spurning Alcyone, Cynthia has upset the orderly pattern of daily existence. The disharmony of the shepherd microcosm is reflected in Nature—Alcyone is no longer a part of the orderly pattern. Night and day are alike for him. He does not go to care for his flock at dawn. Cueva relies on another figure of speech, epiplexis, to set forth the shepherd's grief in a series of rhetorical questions uttered not in order to know, but to provide an emotional release. Alcyone asks when the beloved will respond to the plaintive notes of his flute.

It is worth recalling that in his use of figures of speech, Cueva follows the advice of Doctor Juan Huarte de San Juan. In his book on vocational guidance—*Examen de ingenios para las ciencias* (*A Scientific Classification of Personalities*), published in 1575—Doctor Huarte advises writers to move the audience to emotive heights by use of sententious language and rhetorical devices.[6]

Early in life Juan de la Cueva assured for himself the position of foremost exponent of the epistle. A verse letter usually addressed to a friend, this genre is more doctrinal than lyrical, but is considered here because of the affinity of its classical origins to the more lyric material. From the time of Horace— who is thought to be the inventor—epistles have exerted a forceful influence on Western literature. Some, letters from the Apostles, are included in the New Testament. Expressive of a wealth of ideas, the genre has included lyric descriptions of bygone eras, intimate reflections, even military and political strategy. Others—as, for example, Ovid's *Heroides*—are simply an excuse to air the poet's amorous vicissitudes.

During the first half of the sixteenth century, as we have
seen, Seville produced notable Humanists who translated the
works of Horace and his imitators. Surprisingly, few of the
translators attempted works in the same vein. For example,
Horace was not imitated by Pacheco, Mal Lara, Girón, or Francisco de Medina.[7] The distinction of being the first Horacian
imitator belongs to Juan de la Cueva whose epistles and satirical
works are among his best in the classical tradition.

The epistles reveal a gradual evolution in technique. For
example, the fourteenth, from Pompey's wife Cornelia to Julius
Caesar, is an imitation of Ovid's *Heroides*, and it is the first of
its kind in Spanish.[8] Though the date of composition is unknown, it may well have been an early work. It is but one more
example of Cueva's interest in the hero—in this case, the letter
of a famous lady to a hero. Indeed, much of the energy of the
Renaissance was channeled toward a search for the perfect
heroic poem—a poem that might state the essential truth about
a particular age or generation.

But Juan de la Cueva was a rebellious and often estranged
member of the School of Seville. Curiosity and the tendency to
cast aside the severe criteria of the older generation of his
contemporaries led him to express himself in quite a new type of
epistle. The next phase in Cueva's poetic development is a direct
consequence of the loss of momentum within the Humanist movement. As the crest of the tide of faithful imitation passed, writers
began to depart from the simplicity of classical models and to
insist on a new and imaginative display of elegance. The poet
would become less concerned with simply communicating an
experience. Foremost would be the need to create an intricate
device, a dramatic appeal to the ear. Concurrent with the shift
of stylistic emphasis was the new thematic preference—a rapid
increase in national awareness. The pure Renaissance apotheosis
of models was increasingly reduced by the proud assertion that
native potential was equal to that of the ancients. In the polemic
between the old formalism and the revisionaries, Cueva sided
with the moderns. Henceforth two tendencies will prevail in his
epistles—histrionics as the foundation stone of his oratory and
pride in Spain's coming of age as a world power. Increasingly,
Cueva's epistles will show his adherence to the doctrines of post-

Renaissance theorists. For example, he followed Pedro Malón de Chaide's advice to poets: make doctrinal works more palatable by sprinkling the raw ingredients with ample portions of verbal gimmicks since "meaty plates must be seasoned with tasty garnishes if the diner is to swallow them."

Three of the epistles—all of which are in tercets, the traditional strophe of the genre—describe Cueva's impressions of Mexico. The ones to Sánchez de Obregón, first Corregidor of Mexico, and to Maestro Diego Girón were written while abroad. The third, to his cousin Andrés Zamudio de Alfaro, was written during the return voyage. Although earlier mention has been made of the epistle to the Corregidor, it deserves further comment for the variety of themes treated. After praising the dedicatee and alluding to the rigors of maintaining order in a foreign land, Cueva claims competence only in the laws governing poetry. Admitting that Mexico has been hospitable to him and that he likes the land, the poet lists his impressions of the city—surprise that it is built up in the middle of a lake, amazement at the tall buildings opulent in their stone and marble construction, and his wonder at the intricate system of irrigation which supplies water to the city. Using an alliterative series of nouns, Cueva summarizes the wonders of the new land that most appeal to him: "Six things outstanding in beauty/ I find written with an *h*/ which are exceptional/ and worth praising for their grandeur:/ houses, highways, horses of great beauty,/ hearty meats, handsome manes, and healthy children,/ each and every one praiseworthy."[9]

Finally, Cueva describes the abundance of exotic new foods which tempt the appetite: the plantain, mammey, guava apple, soursop, sapodilla, avocado, etc. Mocking the squeamish tastes of the foreigner (*cachopín*) who is afraid of gastronomical experiments, Cueva extols such local delicacies as the poultry ragout (*pipián*). Turning to the indigenous population, the author declares that though the Indians are ill-tempered and surly, he enjoys their dances, especially the *mitote*. He is surprised that at their councils they carry no lances or shields, but, instead, use wine jugs discarded by the conquerors to beat out a rhythm for the dancers. Cueva finds the lyrics monotonous, but observes that the song is a native epic—recalling the ill luck, imprisonment, and death of Montezuma. Cueva's candid reflections on Mexico are probably as early as any ever penned. Higenio Capote suspects that this episode inspired Bernardo de Balbuena whose *Grandeza mexicana* (*Mexican Grandeur*) appeared in 1604.[10] Also later is Eugenio de Salazar's "Epistle to Fernando de Herrera," which was written from Mexico.[11]

The remainder of Cueva's epistles treat a great variety of subjects. Two are moral in tone—one argues the superiority of a wealthy fool or a poor genius, and the second preaches that moderation in all things is the greatest virtue. The influence of Horace is notable in both. In others Cueva praises Spanish wines and criticizes those who adulterate their poems with foreign words. In fact, many of the epistles are concerned with literary values. He addresses to the jurist Rodrigo Suárez his thoughts on the risks incurred by poor men who attempt to publish books, and to Herrera a discourse on the excessive liberties being taken in oratory and poetry. He is most virulent in his attack on a mediocre translator of Virgil's eclogues who was not careful to preserve the original meaning. One of the most pleasing epistles is the one to Fernando Pacheco de Guzmán. The praise of the tranquility and freedom from mundane cares which he has found in the town of Aracena recalls the best of Fray Luis de León's harmonious, unadorned verses conceived with sincerity and great feeling. Cueva remarks that his inner peace extends even to include affinities with his rustic neighbors for whom he composes occasional poems in simple, unpretentious language: "Here there is neither a polished forehead, nor hands like ivory,/ no eyes dazzling as stars, nor hair of spun gold,/ instead plain language as to the point as a shriveled hand" (*No hay tersa frente aquí, ni ebúrneas manos,/ ni luces bellas, ni cabellos de oro,/ sino términos gafos y muy llanos*).

Cueva reaches the culmination of his epistolary art in the poem addressed to Diego de Nofuentes de Guevara. It is the most novelesque in spirit, full of amusing situations, witty jokes, and comic descriptions. Menéndez Pelayo observes that one character portrayal bears a marked likeness to the figure of Dómine Cabra, the miserly schoolmaster immortalized in Quevedo's *La vida del Buscón* (*The Life of a Delinquent*).[12]

As has been pointed out, in all of Cueva's lyric works, as well as in the eclogues and epistles, one perceives the depth of his classical heritage. The same themes that interested the poet up until 1582 continue to appear in the later works in manuscript. Otis H. Green, commenting on this fact, states that "it is significant for us, inasmuch as it attests the fact that the author, in 1603, still counted on reader interest in his poetic production of earlier decades, characterized by *courtly* love of have-and-have-not, by *courtly* insistence on secrecy and the disguise of the lady behind the poetic *sennal*, and by *Neoplatonic* insistence on purity and licitness."[13] Particularly in his amatory verse, Cueva shows his imitation of Petrarch and, to a lesser degree, of other Italian writers including Serafino Aquilano and Giraldi Cinthio. Commenting on these influences, Professor Joseph G. Fucilla has summarized Cueva's lyric output as "reflecting all the conventional devices there are in Petrarch's works—themes, concepts, wording and techniques which he cleverly incorporates."[14]

The question arises as to why in 1603 Juan de la Cueva should reproduce in an expanded manuscript version the very poems included in the 1582 edition of the *Works*. Maestro Diego Girón had stated in his preface to the reader that most of the poems selected for inclusion in the *Works* are either heroic or amatory. What is particularly strange, Cueva does not appreciably change the prefatory material of the manuscript. The prologue by Girón describing the contents is the same, as are four of the six laudatory poems: an elegy by Doctor Pedro Gómez, two sonnets by Rodrigo Suárez, and one by Claudio de la Cueva. Girón's remarks are all the more inappropriate with the dedication to Claudio in which Cueva states, "I have culled from my papers this volume composed over the years and for different reasons, omitting the core, which is amatory."[15] Cueva proceeds as if he were preparing for publication not a second printing, but a completely unknown work. In fact, he dares to copy the same six octaves addressed twenty years earlier to Juan Téllez Girón, changing only the name of the dedicatee who here is his brother Claudio. When he called attention to this curious phenomenon, Wulff advanced the rather controversial theory that Cueva's procedure is evidence that the 1582 printing of the *Works* was never circulated.[16] He observed that the edition was printed with a copyright (*privilegio*) for ten years which was issued in Lisbon the 15th of April, 1582. But, to his knowledge, there is no evidence that permission for printing (*aprobación*) was ever granted. Wulff is right in suggesting that, if it could be proved that the *Works* was suppressed or withdrawn from circulation, Cueva's bitter protests against his ill luck would take on new and more comprehensible meaning. It still remains a mystery why Cueva never published this particular manuscript nor the one which he prepared in 1604 and called the "Second Part of the Works of Juan de la Cueva."[17]

The lyrical value of Cueva's poetry extends beyond the confines of the verses discussed already. Variety is always his keynote, and thus it is that even the narrative poetry abounds with examples of poetic skill and originality. Cueva was unable to limit his use of formal mannerisms just to the sonnets and *canciones*, the amorous and doctrinal works. The following excerpt from his epic poem will illustrate Cueva's expertise in transferring lyrical qualities to an essentially narrative genre. The technique of stating parallel examples which are then recapitulated—termed the "summation schema" by Curtius—is one of Cueva's most recurring devices:

> The flowers both fragrant and delicate
> Upon whose grassy carpet he trod,
> The sweet song of unconfined birds,
> Called out to him to rest.
> Yet his purpose and weighty cares
> Kept him steady on his course,
> Which neither flower, grass, tree, bird, or river
> Could sway or slow in the least.

> (*Las flores olorosas y suaves*
> *Que en el yerboso suelo iba pisando,*
> *El dulce canto de las libres aves*
> *A detenerse le iban convidando.*
> *Mas el deseo, y los cuidados graves*
> *Lo llevaban el curso apresurando,*
> *Que ni flor, yerba, árbol, ave, río,*
> *Menguar podían de su curso el brío.*)

Linking poetic theory with his search for a truly heroic literary form, Cueva exhibits a continuity of vision which will be examined in the narrative poetry in the following chapter.

CHAPTER 7

The Narrative Poetry

I   La conquista de la Bética (The Conquest of Andalusia)

A. *Antecedents*

THE historical epic held a remarkable sway over the imagination of writers of the epoch of Philip II. As was the case with the emergence and flowering of Spanish lyric poetry during the sixteenth century, the theoretical justification for longer narrative poems was the concept of mimesis. Italian poets and their Spanish followers—imbued with a thorough appreciation for the subtleties of imitation—strove to emulate the great models of classical antiquity. Consistently they regarded the epic as the highest form of poetic expression—the "sublime" style proclaimed by Aristotle. The Renaissance fervor for translations had made most classic epics accessible in the vernacular.

In Spain the phenomenal burst of development of the erudite epic was characterized by interest in national themes and heroes as well as unabashed pride in the militaristic tenor of life. Further impetus was provided by the publication in 1581 of Torquato Tasso's *Gerusalemme liberata* (*Jerusalem Freed*) which found fertile topsoil in Spain.[1] This work, and the later exposition and defense of the author's epic theories, entitled *Discorsi del poema epico* (*Essays on Epic Poetry*), profoundly influenced Spanish writers for generations. In Tasso was found the precedent to permit the intensification of an already emerging religious undercurrent. Henceforth, the conquering heroes of the Spanish epic would behave less as worldly princes and more as Christ's chosen captains defending the Faith.

A brief sampling of the *potpourri* of historical epics which antedate Cueva's *Bética* is sufficient to indicate the popularity of the new genre. In 1586 Pedro de la Vecilla Castellanos published his two-part epic, *El león de España* (*The Lion of*

111

Spain), which traces the origin of the city of Leon. The Estremenian poet Cristóbal de Mesa composed an epic in 1594 entitled *Las navas de Tolosa* (*The Plains of Toulouse*) after having met Tasso while traveling in Italy. Nor did the feats of the greatest national heroes lack for interpretation during this period. Diego Jiménez Ayllón composed the *Famosos y heróicos hechos del Cid* (*The Famous and Heroic Deeds of the Cid*) in 1568, and the exploits of Bernardo del Carpio were recounted repeatedly by diverse poets between the years 1555 and 1625. Other more contemporary heroes, both national and foreign, were the subjects of poems—Charles V, Don Juan of Austria, and Sir Francis Drake. With such a variety of precedents, it is only natural that literary historians should have disagreed on the influence of Tasso on Cueva's work. More certain is the probable influence as a source of historical data of the *Crónica del Santo Rey don Fernando* (*The Chronicle of His Majesty Ferdinand the Saint*) which was published at Salamanca in 1540 and reprinted twice at Seville, in 1550 and 1576.

Regrettably, execution rarely equaled conception, with the result that many of the spate of historical epics have long been forgotten. While from a literary point of view the amount of praiseworthy poetry contained in these epics is lamentably small, it must be conceded that the relaxation of heretofore strict norms of composition occasionally produced felicitous results. A deliberate vitiation of form permitted the inclusion of digressions and novelesque interpolations which in part alleviate the tedium of the unnatural bombastic language. Whatever the current consensus regarding these works might be, we must remember that they were eminently popular in their time, and that they were read seriously by other poets as late as the eighteenth century. Incredible as it may seem, Cueva's often berated poem was judged by one prominent critic to surpass even the religious dramas of Calderón.[2] If for no other reason than this, the time has come to remove the brushwood with which conflicting aesthetics have surrounded the work.

B. *Summary and Analysis*

The *Conquest of Andalusia* is Cueva's longest and most ambitious work. Divided Homerically into twenty-four cantos, the poem consists of more than ten thousand verses in royal octaves. The cantos are unequal in length. The introductory pages of the princeps editicn contain an impassioned eulogy to Seville which was deleted in the Ramón Fernández edition of 1795.

Cueva plunges into his subject with *gran gusto*, seemingly determined to overcome the obstacles which, by its nature, the epic requires the poet to surmount. In the words of Cueva's apologist,[3] the epic poet must create:

a tableau to represent either the fall or the foundation of an empire which is the product of an exceptionally superior human being—a tableau in which will be raised to the foreground grandiose men, strong passions, frightful obstacles of an epoch which bequeaths to posterity majestic rituals, the laws and customs of a great nation. To achieve grandeur in the least significant details of the portrayal, without seeming inflated or grotesque, all the disparate parts of the whole should appear harmonious, each seeming original and novel. Wonderment must be produced without straining the credibility of the reader. The poem must be conceived in a noble, pure diction that is beautifully harmonious, lively and descriptive.

Whether or not Cueva succeeded in adhering to these stringent guidelines has been debated for centuries. There can be no question but that he hoped to emulate the most perfect models of his predecessors. The action is extensive and, for the most part, interesting. The epoch selected—the thirteenth century— was the greatest of the Spanish Reconquest. His intention was to describe the injuries imposed on Spain by the Saracens, recount their expulsion from Andalusia—and Seville in particu- lar—and herald the reestablishment of Christianity in their stead. The hero of the war was the best those centuries could produce. Under Ferdinand III, Castile and Leon pressed deeper into Moorish territory which the magnanimous ruler would grant to the nobles who assisted him in the crusade. The zeal, strength, and generosity of Ferdinand were well known. What had been with other conquerors mere ambition to acquire land, became with Ferdinand an obligation to protect the public welfare. His tender humanity and purity of habits were legendary.

He is portrayed as the spiritual leader of Christians known for their virtuous militarism, simple customs, and their near-

fanatical pride in successive victories over the infidel. The
opposite pan of the balance is equally weighted. The Moors,
while in decline, were rich in skills of warfare and counted on a
huge population which was continually reinforced from Africa.
In this stalemate, the genius of a single man was needed to give
one or the other of the two nations a decisive victory. This
"hero" was Ferdinand III, who with his superior attributes
inclines the balance in favor of the Christians, and the Moors
would never again rise from their defeat.

Surprisingly, Cueva shifts the highlight away from the Christian camp early in the poem. Tangential intercalated stories
of tragic love affairs among the Moors constitute the major
interest of the poem. Individual jealousies and feuds gradually
supplant the greater ideological conflict to command the foreground. As had Tasso, Cueva suppressed scenes of vivid action
in order to expand the rôles of disinterested noncombatants who
—through no fault of their own—became inextricably bound up
in the conflict. Just as Tasso had blown up out of proper
proportion the rôles of Rinaldo and Tancredo, so too did Cueva
accentuate the rivalry of Botalhá and Muley. The influence of Tasso is especially noticeable in the portrayal of the
female characters. Tarfira is unmistakably the counterpart of
Clorinda,[4] and her romantic vicissitudes provide the framework
which unifies a vast number of episodes. Of all the ingredients
which the poet stirs into his epic mixture, the sentimentality of
the Moor is the most striking. Unmistakably the product of an
age of tolerance toward the Moor, the *Conquest* betrays the exotic
appeal of a race no longer universally maligned, but admired
for its gentility.[5]

Book I: The narration begins with the news that the Infante
Alonso has successfully carried out his mission to liberate the
city of Murcia. The King promptly selects Jaén as his next goal,
silencing the dissonant voices of his captains, who disagree on
priorities. The first instance of augury occurs at precisely this
moment, reaffirming the discerning judgment of Ferdinand: an
eagle, bearing in its claws a lamb, descends and flies over the
assembled troops, then flies away. The salient feature of the
beginning of the poem is the tone of discord which provoked
the contempt of generations of critics who regarded dissension

as incompatible with the heroic and lofty purpose of the epic. Cueva's purpose seems to have been to portray the monarch as a wise arbitrator with infinite patience. Many verses are given over to the petty jealousies and bickering of traitorous nobles who appear determined to undermine the crusade. One, in particular, Don Ramiro de Toledo, offers specious loyalty while "striving to further his own personal glory/ but sowing dissension and discord,/ rather than waging honest war."[6] When a loyal peasant flings the truth up to his face, Ferdinand offers his backing in the form of a new title.

Book II: The motif of vengeance is the nexus between the two books. Ramiro is unable to generate interest in his personal cause and learns a moral lesson in humility. Cueva introduces the first minor novelesque digression—which is promptly concluded— to accentuate further Ferdinand's compassion. In the midst of preparations for the siege of Jaén, a young Moor exhibits strange reactions to captivity. His serenity and excessive obeisance prove to derive from relief of his misfortunes rather than guile. He recounts a tale of tragedy which ensued: his elopement with the daughter of the warden of the nearby fortress of Arjona. Pursued by the latter to his home in Jaén, the Moor was helpless to prevent the burning of his house and slaughter of his family. Managing only to escape through a garden into a remote lane, he and his beloved had found no refuge among their neighbors. In desperation, he disguised the girl as a man, and attempted to slip outside the city by night. She fell to her death just before her lover's capture. Ferdinand's compassion is boundless, but he also exploits a tidbit of information inadvertently supplied by the Moor: the confidence of the enemy is based on a hidden source of water which Ferdinand is informed of by the Moor, whose motivation is gratitude instead of the desire for vengeance against his oppressors. At once the King leads a midnight foray up to the walls of the city where the buried pipes are discovered and irreparably damaged after the channel is diverted.

Book III: Here the author approaches the purest epic technique. The narrative rises to a higher intellectual and spiritual level as determined warriors are locked in a costly stalemate. Ferdinand demonstrates his expertise in strategy, shifting heavy scaling machines to attack the weakest wall, and never leaving them unguarded even when the battle subsides at night. The most interesting development arises when an *alfaquí*, an interpreter of the Koran, offers false hope to the Moors in the form of a prophecy. Translating signs seen in the River Guadalbullón, he decrees that the Moors must watch the Christian campfires when a certain object is cast in them. If they die down, the deliverance of the city is assured. A small party descends and approaches the fires, only to be discovered by the guards who repulse them. Before he can be captured, the prophet throws himself into one of the fires and is consumed, to the dismay of the gallery of Moorish spectators. Ferdinand is awakened by the moans of the enemy soldiers lamenting their destiny. When the battle is renewed, the King sends scouts to cut off supply routes from Arjona—only twenty miles away—from which the enemy expects reinforcements.

Book IV: After six days of fierce fighting, part of the fortress wall gives way in the final attack. Jubilation turns to consternation when scouts report the advance of the King of Arjona. Discord tends to rear its ugly head as some captains try to persuade the King to leave off the attack and look toward the new menace. When the King of Arjona reaches the battlefield, he requests a truce in order to surrender as a vassal to the Christian ruler. Tribute is established, and Jaén is opened to the Christians, who reconsecrate the mosque. The Mayor of Jaén severely condemns the treaty and flees in the direction of Seville as night falls on the liberated city. Cueva momentarily returns to the sentimental story of Buyarruz who fears that the emissary of the King of Arjona—whose daughter he had abducted—will demand his extradition. Hamet Golut does, in fact, demand his punishment. Again Ferdinand wisely adjudicates the question without compromising his hospitality to the outcast. It is agreed that the offended father and Buyarruz will meet in hand-to-hand combat in a neutral zone.

Book V: The morning after the entry into Jaén—which fell in 1246 and at once became the advance staging area for successive advances—the Christians admire the architecture of the fortress and city. The tranquility of this fresh April morning is broken when Golut demands that the duel with Buyarruz be fought without delay. With only a cutlass for defense, the young

Moor faces his opponent before a gallery of spectators. Ferdinand's chosen referee objects that the contest is unequal, and Golut's personal bodyguard is paired with Buyarruz, only to fall mortally wounded. Enraged, Golut takes his place and meets the same fate. The King of Arjona rides out to be a third but is stopped by the Christians. At this point Cueva portrays Ferdinand as an angry king who—having been merciful—can also display a vengeful side. Furious at the reports of how Buyarruz addressed his king, the Christian ruler rebukes him soundly for his lack of humility and exiles him for having been disrespectful to his monarch. Unable to find a safe harbor, Buyarruz flees to Seville where he is received by the mayors of that city. The citizens are alarmed because he is armed, and accuse him of being a spy for the Christians, but his story is substantiated by the aged mayor of Jaén who also sought refuge there. Cueva capitalizes on this lull in the action to insert the first paeans to his native city. He resumes the action with the decree of the King of Seville that all Christian prisoners will henceforth be subject to harsh and inhumane treatment. Deep inside their prison caves, the prisoners pray for deliverance. Cueva introduces the motif of the supernatural, describing celestial messengers who appear in the dreams of the sleeping King to warn him of the folly of his decree. When he requests interpretations of his nightmares, the body of the renegade who urged repressive measures is discovered dead, without apparent signs of violence.

Book VI: In this canto, Cueva indulges in his favorite literary device—the intermingling of historical narration and personal pride. First the symbolic dream is analyzed. Seville—represented by a lady in chains symbolic of Moslem and Jew—will be restored to Christian rule. Despite the finality of the interpretation, a Greek soothsayer urges resistance since Christians are powerless against fate. The King of Seville prepares for an attack, assigns Buyarruz a cavalry brigade to command, and sends spies to Jaén. One, disguised as a Christian because he speaks Castilian, is recognized by Cueva's ancestor, the young Lope Díaz de Alfaro, one of the Christian captives. Breaking his chains, he slips away to pursue the spy for three days. The author indulges in a lyric interlude at this point, describing an idyllic

scene as the tracker pauses momentarily on the banks of the
Genil where he succumbs to the attraction of a delightful oasis.
The river, bending nearly 360 degrees, has isolated an island
paradise replete with alders, plantains, water lilies, and roses.
In this desert paradise lives a toga-clad prophet, crowned with
laurel, who lists the illustrious progeny who will add further
glory to an already heroic lineage. He predicts that the young
soldier will succeed in his mission to warn Jaén and will return
to Seville to establish his house from which will spring two men
of exceptional value—one will follow the calling of Mars and
the other that of Apollo. Cueva refers here to his cousin, Francisco de Zamudio de Alfaro, a Knight of the Order of Calatrava,
and, immodestly, to himself! Forewarned by the sage, the youth
breaks through the hostile guards at Castro del Río, reaches
Ferdinand's camp, and warns him of the spy and the defenses
at Seville.

    Book VII: The following morning the guards are doubly
cautious but disturbed because the spy has not appeared. In
the midst of the confusion, the interloper tries to gather more
information. Díaz de Alfaro, having recognized him, is allowed
to seize him alone. Once again Ferdinand gives evidence of his
superiority as a soldier. He allows the spy to see the impressive
array of arms, releases him, and sends an army which will
arrive at Seville almost simultaneously. Although some captains
would have preferred to march against Granada, Ferdinand
selects Seville because of its prestige. After a nine-day march,
Carmona—the near-impregnable city of Roman origins on the
outskirts of Seville—is reached. Nearby is a narrow gorge cut
by a river, inacessible except by a narrow path. Here in a cave
lives an anchorite, an aged Christian prisoner allowed to live
in seclusion. Emerging from his isolated cave, he speaks of the
fears of the Moors and of manna from heaven which sustained
him when the villagers denied him provisions. Ferdinand promises to build him a hermitage once Seville is liberated.

    Book VIII: With roughly one-third of the poem completed,
Cueva superimposes—without sacrificing the steady linear movement of the action—the primary sentimental history of Botalhá,
who had been fleetingly introduced in the sixth canto. A Moroc-
can Prince, he had joined the court of Seville to impress King

Axartaf with his manly deeds, but instead fell in love with the King's daughter, Alguadayra. Ferdinand's decision to press the attack on Alcalá de Guadaira prompts Botalhá to ride to the town and attempt to rescue his beloved. Their exodus is cut short by an alert Christian sentry who sounds the alarm, but the fleeing couple eludes their pursuers. Returning to Seville, they cross paths with the third member of the amorous triangle, Muley Bohacén, the cousin of the Infanta, who reproaches her for disregarding her honor. Deaf to her logic, Muley challenges his African rival, who agrees to face him later. After a long siege, Ferdinand subdues Alcalá, which surrenders to his vassal, the King of Granada.

Book IX: The Catholic King returns to his citadel at Carmona, where—to the dismay of the Moors watching helpless inside their *alcázar*—he plunders and burns enemy farms. Finally Carmona and a half-dozen nearby towns accept the Christian terms of surrender. Ferdinand occupies the plains of Seville and sends an army to block advancing reinforcements from Tangier and Ceuta. Cueva turns next to the thickening plot of the rival lovers. Having been sent to summon a sage for the King, Muley implores the magician to implicate his rival when he reads the future. Cueva draws on the supernatural in his description of the fantastic beasts that guard the cave dwelling—gorgons, chimeras, sphinxes, and minotaurs populate the murky passageways. Muley and his guide are made invisible for a stroll through Seville, during which the sight of Botalhá so incites Muley that he tries to kill him. At once the spell is broken, and both men become visible. In the subsequent scene, a soul emerges from hell to accuse Botalhá and the Princess of disloyalty and to predict that they will conspire with Ferdinand to betray Seville. Despite pangs of conscience, Alguadayra sends a maid to bring her lover to the safety of her chambers. Meanwhile Axartaf is perplexed and angered by the presence of the enemy on the plains below. Cueva attempts to portray the King as a cruel tyrant, describing how he flings from the tower his soothsayer whose only transgression was to name the Christian captains whose faces he can recognize.

Book X: The author introduces two new motifs in this canto—the naval battle on the Guadalquivir and—expanding on the secondary plot—the seduced and abandoned lady. Having received word from Seville to approach the city by sea, African vedettes reach Gibraltar and encounter a smaller Christian flotilla on the river. In the ensuing defeat of the Moors, a girl named Tarfira is fished from the water by Abul Hacén, a Tunisian exile to whom she relates the story of her dishonor and abandonment by Botalhá. Importuned by her rescuer who demands her affection, Tarfira persistently avows love for Botalhá. Their conversation is interrupted by the discovery of Abdalac, who has been gravely wounded in the battle. Tarfira tends his wounds and learns that he, too, loves the Princess Alguadayra. The canto is concluded when the river god Betis raises his damp head and prophesies a decisive Christian victory.

Book XI: Maintaining the supernatural tone, Cueva describes the discourse of Muley and a personification of Envy who promises to fulfill the Moors evil desires. Envy reveals the hiding place of his rival and urges a swift attack. Muley—in an obvious imitation of Rodomonte's rage—furiously denounces the deception, alarming Axartaf. The King forces the doors to his daughter's rooms, but discovers that the frightened pair has fled. Rather than betray the knowledge that her mistress has sought refuge in the Christian camp, the maid bites off her own tongue, and Muley tosses her from the fortress walls. Enraged at the unexpected turn of events, Envy awakens King Abenjafón, custodian of the Triana district, and warns him to stop the Christian advance from that quarter. During the subsequent battle, the fugitive lovers reach safety in Ferdinand's camp, where they are received not as prisoners, but as guests.

Book XII: The thread of the action is picked up again in Seville where Tarfira searches in vain for Botalhá. Abdalac's wife, Meleyca, consults a sorceress who reveals his whereabouts. Muley Bohacén leads a sortie of five hundred soldiers to retrieve the Princess. Depicted as a forceful, headstrong fighter for her honor, Tarfira dons men's clothing and armor in order to accompany the entourage in disguise. In his most masterly treatment of charged emotions, Cueva proceeds to describe the resulting embroilment of mistaken identities and wounded pride in a *tour de force* unequaled in the first half of the poem. Ferdinand consents to a duel between Botalhá and Muley which is interrupted by the disguised Tarfira. Both men claim victory. When the girl's true identity is discovered, she is placated by Lope Díaz de Alfaro, who argues that Botalhá's apparent disregard for her has another explanation.

Book XIII: In the second half of the epic, it is again the amorous conflict that dominates, seeming at times to override the heroic action and seize tonal control of the narrative. Indeed, the erotic conflict provides the basic energy of the work. Axartaf sends Buyarruz to the Christian camp to rescue Tarfira, who is found in the company of an old Moor named Zahen who had offered to help her. She is accidentally knocked unconscious by a falling beam, after which she is escorted back to Seville. The sensibilities of a small group of soldiers are offended by the treatment of the helpless girl. Urging that more fitting deeds be undertaken, several break away from the group and ambush two Christian soldiers. One flees, leaving behind his companion, Garcipérez de Vargas. Cueva's artistry is abundantly displayed in the description of Vargas' extraordinary bravery as he takes on the enemy warriors single-handed before the admiring gaze of Ferdinand.

Book XIV: His vitality noticeably dwindling, Axartaf plots to set fire to the enemy fleet by releasing barges of flaming tar and pitch. Before the plan can be executed, the Christian prisoners ignite the rafts and escape from the city in the confusion. A corresponding resurgence in the secondary plot is notable. Muley Bohacén falls in love with Tarfira and swears eternal devotion to her, thus considering the Princess' slight avenged.

Book XV: In anticipation of a second naval encounter, Ferdinand readies his ships for the imminent victory. Axartaf bitterly watches the massacre of his countrymen from the Tower of Gold.

Book XVI: As the raging battle reaches a crescendo of violence and horror, Muley falls mortally wounded. The Tunisian Hacén —still in love with Tarfira—sees a chance to deceive Axartaf. Rending his dress and tearing his coat of mail, he kneels before the King, his face smeared with blood, to concoct phantasmagorical visions. He claims to have been deposited in the royal palace by a bearded man who appeared to him on a cloud in the midst of the battle and ordered him to denounce Tarfira as the cause of the Moorish defeat. Cueva intrudes on the narration to insert the essential elements of doctrinal content, which may be considered the leitmotif of all of Cueva's works: The poet is unable to conceal the gall of nonrecognition which creeps into all his writings:

> From this deception many wrongs derive,
> And many evil men are favored;
> Just as the good and the loyal are mistreated,
> The deceitful and dishonest are rewarded.
> Honors and high offices
> Go to these, and these are received openly,
> While virtue, loyalty and nobility are
> Treated with scorn and rudeness.
>   (*The Conquest of Andalusia,* fol. 280)

The theme of injustice articulated here is then translated into action. Axartaf praises the lying exile, rewards him, and urges that Tarfira be found. The expiring Muley breathes his last breath defending her from Hacén. Tarfira barely escapes being raped and strangled by the crazed Tunisian. In still another concession to the supernatural, Cueva has Muley rise from death to denounce the assailant to the King. This canto provides an unexpected monologue in which Muley recounts his sensations while dying: a divine spirit guided his soul to heaven. The celestial landscape is one of valleys and springs where the soul observes eight columns of alabaster and gold, resplendent with mosaics and Ionic volutes, supporting a roof studded with precious stones. Symbolic rites of purification in a celestial fountain wash away Muley's humanity before he is sent to warn his uncle of the deception. The message spoken, the lifeless form of the Moor collapses. Hacén's punishment is swift and cruel. He is found by the Christians outside Seville hanging by one foot from a tree, suffocated by his own blood.

   Book XVII: Cueva turns now to reflect the decline of morale in the Christian camp, where discord and envy again threaten the holy enterprise. Ferdinand's captains engage in petty bickering over the superiority of each one. Vainglory stirs three knights to ride out without authorization to attack the gates of Seville, whereupon Ferdinand is obliged to aid them. Although victory follows, the knights are imprisoned for their audacious conduct.

Book XVIII: Dissension prevails as the knights argue how best to persuade their ruler to pardon the jailed men. Cueva affords the reader further glimpses of the King's humanity as the spokesmen approach. Despite his inner sorrow, Ferdinand "disguises his hidden thoughts with a happy countenance,/ appearing amiable to all, a feat that is nearly impossible/ when one is troubled." Encouraging his men to speak openly, he finally acquiesces, and the assemblage gives way to heartfelt rejoicing. Magic adds further variety to this canto. The custodian of the newly-constructed hermitage brings news that a group of Moors has tried to force the burial of one of their number on the grounds. Immediately the Virgin causes them to be transfixed to the ground as a violent storm spews fire from the sierra which consumes the infidels and purifies the spot. Finally, Axartaf sends a spy to Ferdinand's camp who returns to report that so many Christians have been assigned to diverse missions that the camp is practically deserted.

Book XIX: Cueva prepares to retell the fall of Seville. Ferdinand readies his men to attack the Triana Bridge during a series of night maneuvers. The descriptions of gory hand-to-hand combat on the decks of the grappled ships are the most vivid of the epic. Betis surges from the crimson froth to aid the outnumbered Christians. The dynamism of the canto wanes with the recitation of all the heroes who perished in the battle.

Book XX: Ferdinand unites his army with that of the Master of Euclés, who relates the battles he has fought in another sphere. Scouts report that—encouraged by the spy Marsiloro—Axartaf is preparing to leave the city. The Moorish king is deeply disturbed by another vision of Muley whose bloodied face is so mutilated that he is not immediately recognized. This apparition occurs to warn the Moors that Fate is adverse and the attack must be without delay. Cueva shifts attention away from the resulting battle for Triana to the secondary plot. Tarfira confronts Botalhá fully armed and is saved from death by Marsiloro. The latter has a horse that he has trained to bite his adversaries, but Botalhá severs the head of the animal and kills its owner.

Book XXI: Ferdinand's army meets a contingent of troops under the command of his sons, who have been subjugating the Moors of Murcia. The King celebrates the unexpected reunion by ordering a great feast. Seeing that the King would relax the siege, the spirit of Seville's illustrious encyclopedist-bishop, St. Isidore (d. 636), descends to urge unrelenting warfare. Isidore cautions that the war has been protracted because the Christians have not been sufficiently arduous in the crusade. Alguadayra shyly asks permission to speak, and tells the assembled knights that the Moorish strength derives from the favor of the virgins Justa and Rufina, whose names Axartaf invokes in battle and in whose honor he has erected a temple. Ferdinand prays to the Virgin Mary to resist this power and receives an answer through an intermediary, the virgin Palestina, who promises victory. While Ferdinand batters the bridge of Triana, an old Moor urges Axartaf to surrender, reminding him of the ill omens he has seen. Surprisingly, in the face of victory, Ferdinand suffers a momentary reversal. The wind dies down, and his ships are becalmed. Astounded, the Christians throw down their arms, and their monarch prays that his overconfidence be forgiven. Shamed by his humility, the soldiers pick up their arms and prepare to destroy the bridge with their bare hands if necessary. The wind suddenly rises, signaling a victory. The bridge is shattered by repeated assaults with an armored prow, and Ferdinand marches triumphant into Triana.

Book XXII: In this canto, Cueva depicts the chaos which rules in Seville moments before the city is liberated. The Moors are hounded relentlessly. Those who counsel surrender are hacked to pieces by their fanatical countrymen. Spies swim back and forth bringing discouraging reports from Triana. Marsiloro murders Buyarruz and, in turn, is quartered alive by the King. The royal guards are hard pressed to restore order. Thoroughly shaken by the cataclysm, Axartaf opts for peace and sends his elderly cousin Salimo to negotiate with the Christians.

Book XXIII: At dawn the doors of Seville swing open. The terms of surrender are discussed. Ferdinand is again depicted as a reasonable, merciful conqueror: the citizens are allowed to keep their personal property, are treated with dignity, and are even provided safe conduct should they desire to return to Africa.

Ferdinand imposes a one-week terminus for the evacuation. Fittingly, it is Cueva's ancestor, Lope Díaz de Alfaro, who places the Christian standard on the castle tower. As the Moors prepare their exodus, Axartaf's cousin, Salimo, throws himself from the tower and narrowly misses the Infante.

Boox XXIV: The highlight of the concluding canto is Ferdinand's entry into Seville and his wonder at the marvels of the city which he observes from her towers. The deadline having been passed, the Moors still show no signs of their intention to vacate the city. Ferdinand recrosses the river and joins the rest of his army. The Moors believe that he plans to disavow the treaty, but Abdalac explains to Axartaf why the Christians are impatient. Ferdinand grants an extension when Axartaf contends that his people require additional time to dispose of possessions which they cannot carry away. Cueva ends his long epic with the somewhat ambiguous resolution of the sentimental secondary action. Seeing Botalhá a convert in the enemy camp, Tarfira is determined to avenge her dishonor. She rides out fully armed to confront her enemy but is intercepted by a Christian knight who knows her misfortune and pities her. She is brought before Ferdinand who seats her at his side. Cueva remarks that the wise monarch—aware of the importance of his decision—is inspired by heaven to do justice and, at the same time, satisfy the crowd. Mesmerized by the presence of the King, Tarfira requests Christian baptism and the ceremony begins. Experiencing a miraculous change of heart, Botalhá stops the procession and declares his love for Tarfira, but no reconciliation is forthcoming. The reborn Tarfira remains in the court, and Botalhá returns to his kingdom in Africa.

Ambivalence, inconstancy, dividedness: these are the curiously effective sources from which Cueva derives poetic energy for his national saga. The basic erotic and sentimental schemes were conceived to balance the grim tableau of a land in extreme turmoil. As would be expected, the poet chose a metaphorical language that would reflect the same tonal dichotomy. Indeed, the most often repeated device is the imposition of pagan mythology on the limiting epic framework. For example, in the attack on Jaén, the fall of a Moor from the parapet suggests to the poet a wide range of mythological counterparts which he states in an almost Gongoristic style:

> Less noisy was the fall
> of the cruel giant, hurled down to hell
> by Saturn's powerful son [Zeus], who
> waged war against proud Olympus;
> Less terrible was the fiery bolt of lightning
> which darting and falling,
> made a horrible and frightening crash
> as it struck the crag of Atlas' lofty summit.

> (*No cayó con ruido semejante*
> *Del hijo de Saturno poderoso*
> *Derribado al infierno el cruel gigante*
> *Que movió guerra al cielo glorioso;*
> *Ni de la cumbre excelsa de Atlante*
> *Herido el duro risco del fogoso*
> *Rayo, que removiéndose y cayendo*
> *Hace un horrible y admirable estruendo.*)

II   Coro febeo de romances historiales
(Phoebean Chorus of Historical Ballads)

A.   Antecedents

Spain's most respected literary historian of the modern age observed that during the sixteenth century the printing presses of Seville were most frequently engaged in printing ballads.[7] The *romance* (ballad)—which has stirred the emotions of virtually every stratum of society for centuries—is usually considered to be the most popular and representative verse form of all times. Attempts both to define the type and to establish the origins of the ballad have occupied scholars in what is certainly the most difficult question in Spanish literary history. Although it is found in other literatures, there are several peculiar features which appear unique to the Spanish ballad. It is an epico-lyric hybrid of fixed metrical form—relatively short strophes of indeterminate length written in verses of eight syllables, the even-numbered ones having assonant rhyme. It is now thought by most scholars that the earliest ballads—although anonymous—were composed by a single poet whose identity is unknown because his song was considered the property of both the minstrel who disseminated it and his audience. Because of its status as common patrimony of an oral tradition, a single theme was especially suited for improvisation by successive generations of minstrels who would add new versions to an everchanging repertory.

It is customary to classify Spanish ballads according to their subject matter, but, at times, the dividing lines tends to be ill-defined. The largest single body—the primitive ballads (*romances viejos*)—recalls the deeds of characters who are so well known that only the essential information is mentioned: the Cid; Roderick, the last Visigoth ruler of Spain; Bernardo del Carpio, the national hero who supposedly lost his life in the Battle of Roncesvalles. The oldest of this type are generally called border ballads (*romances fronterizos*) because they relate the events of border struggles between Christians and Moors up until the fall of Granada in 1492. These are thought to be the oldest because these "news-bearing" ballads were probably sung very soon after the events narrated took place.

Ballads of this type, as well as those whose origin is the French Carolingian material, were first printed singly or in groups of fewer than six on broadsides or *pliegos sueltos* from about the year 1500. Since the unbound sheets were so perishable, few survived for long. The years immediately prior to Juan de la Cueva's birth were especially significant for the *romancero* or ballad anthology. Between 1545 and 1550 the first extensive collection devoted exclusively to ballads was printed by the House of Martín Nucio in Antwerp. Called the *Cancionero de romances sin año* (*Undated Songbook of Ballads*), it was followed by an amazingly large number of similar collections which appeared at the rate of nearly one annually for the next one hundred years.

At about the same time as this landmark in the printing of ballads, there occurred still another development in the history of the genre. Seeking inspiration in Renaissance treatises on poetics which exalted narrative poetry, Spanish writers attempted to refurbish the primitive ballads and compose original ones. These new erudite ballads (*romances eruditos*) were, for the most part, based on the historical prose accounts found in

Spanish chronicles, for example the *Crónica de España* (*Spanish Chronicle*) published by Florián de Ocampo in 1541. Proud of their new artistic ballads—as they are sometimes called—and anxious that they not be considered mere pastiches, these poets shunned anonymity in what amounted to a rush for recognition. While at first they favored historical themes, by 1587—the year in which Cueva published his own collection—the vogue had already shifted to a taste for two new varieties, the Moorish and the pastoral. Both types were clearly conceived to be read rather than sung. Likewise, they soon evolved to include parody and satire as well as thinly-veiled autobiographical anecdotes. The first editions of this new ballad form began to be published about the year 1585 and bore such titles as *Flor de Romances* (*Bouquet of Ballads*), *Rosas de Romances* (*Corsage*) or simply *Silva* (*Miscellany*).

B. Summary and Analysis

The *Coro febeo de romances historiales* (*Phoebean Chorus of Historical Ballads*)—Cueva's contribution to the fast-growing aggregate of artistic ballads—was dedicated to Juana de Figueroa y Córdoba. She was the mother of his friend and contemporary, Gerónimo de Montalvo, a Knight of the Order of Santiago and Mayor of Seville. Published in November of 1587, this *romancero* is the author's second-longest work. It comprises ten divisions, each dedicated to one of the muses. Lacking one, Cueva called his dedicatee the tenth muse. The work is further divisible into topics from Spanish history and the histories of foreign empires —Greece, Rome and Asia Minor, as well as biblical stories. A second collection of ballads conceived along the same lines never progressed further than the manuscript stage.[8] The published part contains many more ballads on Spanish subjects than does the incomplete sequel. The second part concentrates particularly on Virgilian motifs, one ballad recounting the course of the Trojan War from beginning to end. The *Chorus* is but another of Cueva's inaccessible works, fewer than half a dozen copies of the princeps edition being known to exist. Sixty-two of the ballads were rescued from obscurity in the nineteenth century when Agustín Durán included them in his very representative *Romancero general* (*General Collection of Ballads*).[9]

The Cuevan interpretation of history is largely conventional, as are the classical sources which influenced his selection of ancient myths. Although he writes of Greek history, the majority of the isolable models are Latin poets. Menéndez Pelayo credited Cueva with the distinction of introducing into Spanish literature the story of the Golden Ass which ultimately harks back to Apuleius' *Metamorphoses*.[10]

The *Chorus* has received almost no critical comment in the twentieth century. Arturo Marasso weakly suggests that the ballad about Timon of Athens might have been inspired by the Greek Anthology (*Epigrammatum Anthologia Palatina*) which he states is the only Greek source frequently consulted by Golden Age poets.[11] Professor Edwin S. Morby cites the considerable influence of Ovid's *Metamorphoses* on the ballads treating the following topics: the dispute of Ajax Telamon over Ulysses' weapons, the rescue of Andromeda from death by Perseus, the desertion of Ariadne by Theseus, and the ballads about Nisus, Scylla, Minos, and Pasiphaë.[12] Other discernible borrowings are from Lucan, Horace, Statius, Xenophon, Herodotus, and Plutarch.[13] José María de Cossío's study of Spanish versions of mythological fables scarcely scratches the surface of the *Chorus*. He singles out only one, the ballad of Ajax Telamon, from the great number of myths treated by Cueva.[14]

Without exception, the judgments pronounced on these ballads have been negative. Even Durán qualified his inclusion of a sampling of them, which he harshly condemned as deficient in taste and sensitivity. In all honesty, it must be admitted with regret that Cueva's Renaissance-inspired compulsion to try his hand at nearly every genre was, to say the least, a hazardous enterprise. Reassessed, the *Phoebean Chorus* affords no satisfaction nor reveals any redeeming qualities. Lamentably, these ballads deserve only to be consigned to that body of writings that is best forgotten.

CHAPTER 8

The Poets' Guide

AS the preceding chapters have shown, Juan de la Cueva was a writer whose creative instincts led him to explore many literary paths in his conquest for personal fulfillment. It was inevitable that Cueva should be drawn into the greatest literary polemic of the Golden Age. That he would feel compelled to state his position in a formal treatise was equally predictable.

One of the most far-reaching ramifications of the entire Renaissance-Humanist movement in Spain was the awakening of interest in classical theories of composition. When, in 1596, Alonso López Pinciano published his *Filosofía antigua poética* (*Ancient Theory of Poetry*), the battle lines had already been formed. An entire generation of writers would engage in emotional—and not always tasteful—attacks on fellow theorists who dared to disagree with their literary precepts.[1] At the core of the polemic was one basic question: the validity of an art unencumbered with rules. El Pinciano, as López was called—and his followers, the neo-Aristotelians—insisted upon strict adherence to the precepts dictated by Aristotle, Horace, and Plato. As the controversy grew, it tended to revolve around the dispute over the directions that the national drama was taking in Spain. On the one hand, the defenders of Lope de Vega espoused complete freedom from classical restrictions in the drama, while on the other, uncompromising advocates of formal poetics condemned any work not conceived in the purest classical spirit.

Facing lines so clearly drawn, Juan de la Cueva found himself in a somewhat unenviable position. The esoteric and noble in literature had been for him a constant lure. He took pride in imagining himself part of a select minority of discreet writers whose guiding principles were decorum and propriety. Yet he knew that, in the strictest sense, his works could not be made

130

to fit into rigorous classical molds. He had taken too many liberties with the rules, and now he faced one of two alternatives—recantation or reaffirmation of practices forged during a lifetime of writing. Understandably, Cueva's attempt to straddle the controversial questions of the day resulted in equivocal statements and contradictions in his theories.

Cueva's treatise on literature, the *Ejemplar poético* (*Poets' Guide*), was never published during his lifetime. The earliest version of the work appears in an autograph manuscript dated 1606 and is dedicated to his patron, Enríquez de Ribera.[2] Clearly the raging conceptual debate was uppermost in his mind during his last years, and he wanted this formal declaration of his own position to be as contemporary as the everfluctuating consensus. To this end, Cueva revised and corrected the manuscript several times between 1606 and 1609—the date of the definitive version.[3] The *Guide* was first published by López de Sedano, who purported to use for his edition still another manuscript now lost.[4] The most reliable modern edition is that of E. Walberg, which is accompanied by a lengthy analysis and study of the sources of Cueva's poetics.[5] This scholar accurately assesses the value of the document as twofold: first, Cueva's position with regard to the drama and, second, the historical importance of being the first original statement of literary precepts written in Spanish.[6]

A word should be said concerning the originality of the *Poets' Guide*. Horace's *Letter to the Brothers Piso*—commonly referred to as his "Art of Poetry"—was first translated into Spanish in 1591 by Vicente Espinel.[7] Through this and later translations, the Horacian ideology directly influenced the critical standards of Cueva and his contemporaries. Cueva's *Guide* is, in fact, the earliest Spanish imitation of Horace's *Epistle,* but this is not to say that it is slavishly faithful to it from beginning to end.

The *Poets' Guide* is composed in tercets, and it is divided into three sections which Cueva calls epistles. In the first, he dwells on general discussions of literature and literary theory, alluding in turn to many of the questions currently being argued. The second treats specifically Spanish verse—its origins, techniques, and superiority over other foreign forms. Finally, in the third section, Cueva addresses himself more specifically to the question of the drama.

Cueva's arguments in the *Guide* can be reduced to the Aristotelian doctrines of imitation of nature and verisimilitude. His understanding of probable-seeming literature is the same as that expressed by Horace. He explains that the function of the poet is not to limit himself to a faithful reconstruction of a past or present reality. Rather, what he depicts must be sufficiently credible so that—even if it is merely fictitious invention—it could pass as history because of its believable semblance (I, 235-43).[8]

In this view, Cueva reiterates the Aristotelian distinction between the poet and the historian. The poet's realm is fiction, and his vehicle is verse. Because his works are fabrications, or lies, he has an even greater responsibility to pretend that his product is the truth, for the value of fiction is upheld only if it retains a modicum of reality (I, 250-79). On the other hand, prose is the medium exclusively reserved for historical truth. The historian, then, must avoid at all costs interpretations of reality. The validity of his work resides precisely in its objectivity.

What, then, is the supreme goal of literature according to Cueva? He repeats the Aristotelian tenet that rejects "art for art's sake" in favor of a literature conceived with a didactic or moral purpose. Poetry should not be written for pure aesthetic enjoyment alone, but must also edify. If it does not instruct, it is valueless (I, 292-309).

Cueva's aesthetic theory is relatively unassuming. He states that successful poetry does not result from verse harmony and grandiloquent words alone (I, 40-72). Rather, individual poetic intuition and a true feeling for style must combine and go hand in hand to form a work of art. One without the other is not sufficient to produce art (I, 91-120).

The opinions expressed about the acceptable poetic lexicon are of particular interest since Cueva's own poems indicate that his execution was not always equal to the conception. He cautions against using pompous language and words difficult to comprehend (I, 79-90). Likewise, in order to avoid inverisimilitude, the selection of vocabulary should be appropriate to the subject being treated (I, 163-92). Nobles and heroes should not speak in language that would demean their status in life, and the lowborn should not be heard expressing lofty conceits.

Cueva's view concerning the use of neologisms is especially
important in the light of his attitudes toward Gongoristic excesses. He stresses more than once the need to enrich the vernacular language with borrowings from the Latin and Greek
lexicons (I, 121-62). It will be remembered that—under the
guise of consoling a fellow poet whose works had been criticized—Cueva had taken issue with his contemporary, Fernando
de Herrera, whose lexicographical improprieties in his *Commentary on Garcilaso* he mocks.[9] More specifically, in the *Guide*
Cueva condemns a variety of grammatical usages which he finds
inadmissible in good poetry: hiatus or interruption of the continuity of thought, a noun modified by more than two adjectives,
and the use of a gerund as an adjective (II, 478-501).

Essentially, it is Cueva's argument that Spanish verse is capable
of being as satisfying, as lofty, and as beautiful as poetry written
in any other language (II, 37-42). He singles out as particularly
lyrical the Spanish couplet (*copla*), whose origin he traces to the
Greek and Latin trochee (II, 49-51). His observations on epic
poetry, which he calls *romance*, are of special interest because he
consistently refrained from using this verse form in his plays.
He theorizes that the Spanish epic is of Visigothic origin and
says that it is very similar to the native equivalents of Greece and
India—the rhapsodies and the *areitas* (II, 136-38). However,
Cueva cautions that under no circumstances is it permissible to
write in a mixture of languages for which he reproaches Garcilaso
de la Vega (II, 295-303).

There is included in this section of the *Guide* an analysis of
the functions and limitations of specific verse forms and poetic
genres. Blank verse requires unusual skill in composition because of its freedom from rhyme which must be compensated
for internally by eloquent expression of varied interest (II, 217-
28). Cueva discusses other verse forms in his remarks on the
drama in the third epistle. We are told, for example, that the
octave is especially suited for the composition of epics and for
use in the drama, where it is ideal for long narrative speeches
(III, 94-108). Actually, Cueva gives his readers a rather free
hand in the use of poetic strophes. For example, he goes on to
concede that the octave, as well as other strophic choices, can
be just as readily used as catchalls, employed to express love

emotions, mockery, laughter, scorn, and sorrow in a wide range
of genres that includes eulogies, epitaphs, and descriptive monologues (III, 109-11). He does insist however—and this is fundamental to his treatise—that the poet must distinguish between
the low and the high styles of poetic expression (III, 103-5).

Menéndez Pelayo was the first to establish that Cueva's discussion of metrics is modeled almost entirely on the theories
of another native of Seville, Gonzalo Argote de Molina, a leading
member of the neo-Aristotelian camp.[10] A dedicated Humanist
and historian, he included with his 1575 edition of the *Conde
Lucanor* a prologue entitled *Discurso sobre la poesía castellana*
(*Discourse on Castilian Poetry*). His observations—which are not
original—on the hendecasyllabic verse are especially important
since Cueva's misconception that the Spanish use antedates the
Italian (II, 154-56) is due to his reliance on the *Discourse*. Cueva
repeats the earlier assertion of Argote that López de Mendoza,
the Marquis of Santillana, was the first Spaniard to compose
verse in this meter (sonnets). And, according to Menéndez
Pelayo, the writers of the School of Seville were apparently alone
in their knowledge that sonnets had been written in Spanish
before the sixteenth century.

Cueva does not state that his observations on metrics are new.
But, at the same time, he acknowledges dependence only on
Aristotle, Horace, and their Italian commentators—Scaliger,
Giraldi Cinthio, and others (II, 541-49).

One section of the *Poets' Guide* has been of more than routine
interest to scholars. In the first epistle (vv. 373-544), Cueva
refers to an anonymous poet who tried his hand at many different genres and in particular the epic. Instead of achieving a
lofty, sublime style, he produced only insipid lines in which he
expressed lowly thoughts. Advised of his shortcomings by friends,
the poet realized his lack of eloquence. Calling upon Apollo for a
revelation of his faults, he demanded to know why his work is
inferior and how he could insure proper recognition for his
efforts. While asleep, his true intellect was aroused by the
muses. Upon awakening, the poet gathered together the combined works of his youth—once so jealously defended—and threw
them to the flames. His creative instincts were revived in works
for which his temperament was best suited. We are told that

he renounced forever both tragedy and comedy, as well as epic and lyric poetry. He turned instead to a humble but gratifying project: to tell the history of his lineage and origins in Seville, and "the composition of verses about ordinary people, lacking heroic proportions and pretension."

Cueva's theory of following one's natural inclination and the concept that not all poets are endowed with the genius to compose all kinds of poetry is still another example of a tendency towards retraction in the *Guide*. Walberg was convinced that the anonymous poet could be none other than Cueva himself,[11] and —in all fairness—it must be admitted that the textual allusions would seem to support his view. If this sketch is, in fact, autobiographical, it must be understood that during a fit of depression Cueva decided to reject the value of the works of his early years. This would certainly explain why he decided not to publish the second volume of his plays which we know he planned to send to the press, as well as account for the fact that the second collection of his mythological ballads was allowed to remain in manuscript. The geneological poem referred to is clearly his own *History and Issue of the Cueva Family*. Yet not all are convinced that Cueva referred to himself in these lines. Guerrieri Crocetti took strong exception to Walberg's parallels with Cueva because of inconsistencies between the avowed conversion and the record of published works which Walberg had been unable to account for.[12]

Turning now to the question of the drama, it should be stressed that—in its large sense—the *Poets' Guide* betrays the inner conflict which plagued Cueva during the last years of his life when Lope de Vega was the recognized master of the Spanish stage. Cueva knew that Lope's position was secure and that his brand of drama was preferred to all others by the public. The tone of the *Guide* is tempered by this realization. Consequently, Cueva does not openly insist on the superiority of his plays over those of his rival. He adopts a positive position which—he must have hoped—would insure recognition of his contribution to the definitive form which the seventeenth-century drama, the *comedia nueva*, had acquired. To this end, Cueva defends drama in general and the Spanish *comedia* in particular.

He casts his enthusiasm in the form of a visionary who has

already foreseen and largely contributed to the triumph of the drama. In what comes close to being a palinode, Cueva disavows the authority of classical drama and dramatic precepts and his alignment with their promulgators (III, 520-70). Not only does he condemn the early Spanish drama for its sterile, rigid confines, but he goes so far as to call the classical drama "insipid" (*cansada cosa*). If, he says, he has failed to observe the ancient poetic doctrines, it was because he realized that they were too restrictive and that the Spanish drama could only be elevated through freedom from such encumbrances. The operative word of this section of the *Guide* is "change." Customs and tastes change with time, and what was appropriate in the past is no longer necessarily suitable. Thus it is that he deliberately disregarded the classical authority and allowed restrictions on subject matter and the unity of time to go by the board. Finally, says Cueva, the variety of his drama paved the way for the *comedia nueva* (III, 562-79).

His position is all the more interesting when compared with that of Lope de Vega in his *Arte nuevo de escribir comedias* (*New Art for Writing Plays*), a work which belongs to the same period as the *Guide;* Lope's treatise appeared in 1609. The prevailing dramatic formula which was responsible for his success was dictated—according to Lope—not by his conscience, but by the need to satisfy the demands of an insensitive public that wanted only to be entertained. His tone is—unlike Cueva's—apologetic, as he insists that were he able to choose the public, he would select a learned audience receptive to a superior art form. He does not conceal his disregard for his predecessors, who facilitated the spread of the new dramatic formula. He is especially critical of Lope de Rueda who—according to him—never allowed the drama to rise above a lamentably vulgar level of appeal. It is indeed ironic that Lope—basking in the full glory of success—should have cast a wistful glance back towards the ancients while Cueva—anxious to climb on the bandwagon—purported to disdain them. What is even more startling, although his is an open defense of the new comedy, Cueva fails to allude even once to Lope de Vega in the *Guide*.

Concern that his importance as a dramatist might be insufficiently recognized led Cueva to lay not a few apocryphal

claims to innovative techniques which should be commented upon. In theory, he draws a fine line between tragedy and comedy,
insisting that the former should depict only the deeds of heroes
and royalty, and that the latter should be concerned only with
the lives of ordinary people. Yet he admits that he expanded
the dramatic potential of comedy by blending the genres. He
specifically claims for himself the innovation of introducing
kings and gods in the comedies (III, 505-7). In fact, the practice
is at least as old as the *Comedia Aquilana* of Torres Naharro
which dates from 1524.[13]

Just as imprecise is Cueva's proud boast that he reduced from
five to four the number of acts and renamed them *jornadas*
(III, 508-10). By the midsixteenth century, plays in four and
even three acts had already appeared,[14] and soon Cueva was
not the only dramatist to claim credit for the reduction in number. The term *jornada* was also used by Torres Naharro, who
explained that the pauses in the action were "more than anything
else, stopping places, which allowed the play to be better understood and more easily performed."[15] It is Walberg's rather specu-
lative hypothesis that the word was suggested by the tradition
of the medieval mysteries whose performances lasted several
days, each day being devoted to one act.[16] What is certain,
before Cueva no major playwright after Torres Naharro adopted
the term.

It should be evident from the preceding discussion that the
Poets' Guide is not a treatise easily categorized or evaluated.
On the positive side, it affords in general terms a fairly accurate
statement of the progress of the neo-Aristotelian polemic at the
time that Cueva was writing. Structurally, it is imperfect, marred
by poor organization and repetition. Ideologically, it labels its
author as a fence-straddler anxious to imagine himself a major
contributor to a powerful new vogue while still holding on to
conceptual rudiments of a bygone era.

CHAPTER 9

The Miscellaneous Works

JUAN de la Cueva's humanistic education guided him to explore broad cross sections of the classics. At widely-spaced intervals during his life—in imitation of his preceptors of the School of Seville—he translated or glossed in Spanish a sampling of those compositions which most appealed to his poet's ear. None of these writings was published during his lifetime, and several exist only in manuscript. Though it must be conceded that these works occasionally lack imaginative poetic intuition, it is also true that they manifest a wider balance in Cueva's production than is generally recognized.

I   El viaje de Sannio (Sannio's Journey)

Cueva completed *Sannio's Journey* in Seville on the 16th of June, 1585, and dedicated it to his patron, Fernando Enríquez de Ribera, Marquis of Tarifa. The poem is contained in two manuscripts. One, numbered MS. 82-2-5 of the Biblioteca Colombina, is an autograph and may have been Cueva's rough draft as indicated by the many corrections in the author's hand. The second, MS. 4.116 of the Biblioteca Nacional in Madrid, is a copy of a later date. The only edition of the poem is that of Fredrik A. Wulff.[1]

The poem is divided into five books of unequal length, each with a short prefatory résumé in prose. The versification is royal octaves with the inclusion of a sonnet in the fourth book. Because of its rarity and the light it sheds on Cueva's personal anguish, a summary of the plot is called for.

Sannio, the buffoon of the ancient Greek and Roman mimes, derives his name from *sanna*, a mimic gesture. The archetypal fool and butt of cruel pranks, he and Cueva are here one and the same. The poet's disillusion with his own world prompts him to undertake a journey through the heavens to the throne of Jupiter, of whom he demands recognition for his literary accomplishments and a reward commensurate with his merits. Book One begins with Sannio's dialogue with Virtue, his lifelong companion and the voice of his conscience. He protests that, despite his almost religious respect for discipline and his defense of quality in art, he is "held in low esteem, rejected, his words falling on deaf ears." The poignancy of his acrimonious lament, his desolation and dark weariness result in large measure from the poverty of his external existence. It is regrettable that the wealth and influence of his noble patrons never seemed to be sufficient to protect him from the stark exigencies of daily life.

Virtue is alarmed at Sannio's deep despondency, and tries to discourage him from undertaking so hazardous a journey. Sannio insists and Virtue resignedly serves as his guide. Together they traverse the concentric spheres of the Ptolemaic universe, pushing on to the ninth heaven, the Primum Mobile. In this, Cueva's personal "dark night of the soul," he becomes the most characteristic of baroque protagonists—a pilgrim of pain, lost in the wilderness of frustration and false dreams.

Sannio stands before the celestial gates of Jupiter's realm in Book Two. With indomitable faith in his ideology, he arrogantly calls upon the god to receive him. His words are first heard within by Momus, the god of mockery and censure, who urges Jupiter to punish this impudent meddler in the affairs of the immortal. The father of the gods, irreverently humanized, evades the question because of his gastric indigestion. Judging from Sannio's obstinacy, Momus concludes that he must be either a penniless poet or philosopher and implores Jupiter to refrain from punishing his audacity. It will be remembered that Cueva's *Comedies* and *Tragedies* were dedicated to Momus. When the voice of the poet is finally recognized, Momus seems to change horses in midstream, praising his "lofty and noble intellect." Momus urges that Mercury or Mars be sent as intermediaries to cajole the poet and soothe his ruffled feathers.

What follows in Sannio's debate with Mercury is a curious demythification of the gods of Olympus. Mercury raves and threatens to no avail. Sannio insists implacably that he be admitted. He reduces Mercury to impotent fury with his ironic

references to the sordid side of the immortal's world: incestuous
relations with Cytherea, his sister, the fact that he is sacred
to thieves, etc. Jupiter mobilizes all the deities of Olympus to
expel Sannio. One by one, in Book Three, the gods face the
tranquil poet only to be stripped of their dignity as Sannio throws
in the face of each details of his most reprehensible behavior:
Mars' adultery, Apollo's homicides and delight in unabashed
flattery, Saturn's appalling filicide, Hercules' gluttony and stu-
pidity. He even mocks Bacchus, pulling his staff from under
him, causing the poor fellow to fall. Cupid joins the swarm of
furious gods. Removing his blindfold, he aims an arrow at Sannio,
but the poet remains unperturbed and steadfast in the knowledge
that he is in the right. After all, he is confident that Virtue is
Cupid's sworn enemy. Furthermore, the poet only acknowledges
the sovereignty of pure love, the "chaste Love praised by Socra-
tes and Plato." In repudiation of blind, romantic love, Sannio
grabs an incredulous Cupid and gives him a sound thrashing
with his own bowstring. Pandemonium follows. Venus and Sannio
engage in a furious tug-of-war, Cupid taking the place of a
rope. This book—which with 156 octaves is the longest—ends
in a stalemate. Hercules manages to push shut the doors of heaven
with his massive shoulders before Sannio can slip inside.

In Book Four, Sannio and Virtue await the consequences of
the poet's mockery of the Olympian retinue. The gods and
goddesses throng around Jupiter's throne in alarm, demanding
punishment of the libelous interloper. Unwilling to contravene
Virtue, the deity decrees that Sannio be submitted to an examination by Apollo, who is best qualified to judge his merit. Should
Sannio fail to pass this test, he must suffer the humiliating
caprices of Momus.

The doors swing open, and the unhappy mortal approaches
the throne of the omnipotent to expound on his miseries: "I have
been consistent in following Virtue, and in return I am, as you
see me now, pursued by relentless Hunger. Since you cannot
deny my plight, be merciful, for I only ask that you grant a
reasonable subsistence, because of who you are and on behalf
of the virtue that is my guide."

Jupiter—who never doubts Sannio's destitution—observes
brusquely that if poetry does not provide adequate subsistence,

why then does the poet not try another line of work? Once again the interior debate structure is evident. Are weariness, the ingratitude and deprivation that oblige Cueva to beg for his daily bread so powerful that he must compromise his principles or turn to another profession? Sannio reiterates that his pilgrimage is not for the purpose of proving his worth. Since he has long worn the laurels of Apollo to no avail, the suggestion that his competence be established is absurd. Pressed by Apollo, Sannio defines epic, lyric, elegiac and bucolic poetry, as well as comedy and tragedy—all in accordance with neo-Aristotelian theory.

Finally Apollo asks Sannio whether or not he possesses the qualities which are the prerequisites of a good poet. In support of his enthusiastic "Yes," Sannio recites a sonnet on a classical theme, aware that the outcome of his examination rests on the gods' reaction to it. His poem and an English paraphrase follow:

> *Hirió la trivia diosa en el Leteo*
> *con el tridente del undoso hermano,*
> *por el insulto qu'el pastor troyano*
> *cometió, y suspira el caso Orfeo.*
>   *Apareja Mercurio el caduceo,*
> *árdese en ira Jove soberano,*
> *sin que impida su ánimo inhumano*
> *Juno, ni el tierno abrazo Cytereo.*
>   *Treme el profundo huerco, y del ruido*
> *s'enciende Flegetón, y Febo vuelve*
> *el diurno camino sin gobierno.*
>   *Altérase el parnaso, y conmovido*
> *el zonado zodíaco revuelve*
> *sus doce signos en su curso eterno.*

(The forked river goddess [Oenone] thrust the trident of her wavy brother [Neptune] deep into the River Lethe because of the insult committed by the shepherd of Troy [Paris], and Orpheus laments the event. Mercury menaces with his caduceus, sovereign Jupiter fumes in anger which neither Juno nor the tender embrace of Cytherea can placate. The very bowels of hell shake, and the noise causes the River Phlegethon to burst into flames, and Apollo loses control on his daily run in the sun chariot. Parnassus is in an uproar, and overcome with emotion, the Zodiac juggles the twelve constellations in their fixed orbits.)

A subject less likely to win over the miffed audience is hard to imagine. Sannio appears unconcerned that he is rubbing salt in the already smarting wounds of Olympian pride. While he and Virtue exchange admiring glances, the assemblage erupts in vociferous disagreement. Ironically, judgments are made on the appropriateness of allusions in the sonnet and not on its artistic merit. Neptune naturally admires the "tender, pleasing verses" because the poem expresses the indignation of the gods when Paris abandoned his sister Oenone for Helen. The deciding vote is finally cast by Jupiter, who decrees that henceforth Sannio must be satisfied with virtue alone, for it will be his only recompense. For his efforts, his name will be enshrined in the halls of Fame, but only after his death. In the meantime, he will be subject to envy and hunger. Because he dared insult the gods, he must now be delivered over to Momus for further sentencing.

Momus pronounces an excoriating sentence so all-encompassing that Jupiter has to cut him short with a thunderbolt: "Sannio may never rest, be welcome company, nor find a friend. No one may pity him, nor will his chosen profession ever afford a living. Henceforth he will be known by his threadbare hand-me-downs. Envy will nip at his heels, and his most loyal friends will betray him. His works will be relentlessly criticized." The gods depart, leaving Sannio in spiritual as well as physical solitude.

Book Five is devoted to the spiritual resurgence of Sannio and imparts a cyclical quality to the total tableau with the return of the poet's self-assurance. At first, however, the sense of isolation is complete. He contemplates abandoning himself to the wide path of pleasure and self-degradation, but Virtue promises to remedy his misfortunes.

The pair retraces the steps of the ascent into the heavens to stand once again beside the waters of the Guadalquivir. Sannio—experiencing a psychic transformation—feels waves of tranquility washing over his whole being as he wanders pleasurably, observing the wonderful variety of nature. Virtue sings a touching and highly lyrical paean to Seville and its founders as she leads Sannio to the banks of the river. The pilgrims are met by the nymph Selidonia at whose advance the waters part to reveal a dry path which they follow. An amazing, magical world unfolds before the astonished eyes of the poet. He gazes upon the grotto which is the source of all the Spanish rivers. Betis, King of the rivers, greets the pilgrims cordially and promises Sannio a reward worthy of his sacrifices. But first he must retire to a temple where he will stand in review of mortals who—though the thread of their lives has already been cut by the Fates—are beloved by Fame and by Astraea, goddess of justice who fled the earth when wickedness corrupted the Golden Age. Before Sannio's eyes pass the images of Seville's greatest heroes—men of arms and of letters in equal proportions. The illustrious cortege concludes with the exaltation of a man still living, Cueva's patron, the Duke of Alcalá. The pilgrims observe a statue without a face, cloaked in shadows. They are told that the effigy represents a poet nurtured by envy at the expense of better writers. His nameplate has been obliterated as just punishment for his vanity. There is no clue which would help to identify this Philistine. Cueva's curse of silence was as effective here as that of Cervantes in refusing to name the author of the apocryphal *Quijote.*

Leaving the temple, Sannio is surrounded by sea nymphs, and under the approving eyes of Betis he is solemnly crowned with a laurel wreath and assured that from this day on his adverse fortune will improve. The voice of Betis emanates in new praise of virtue and orders that riches from his undersea treasury be heaped upon the poet. The work concludes as Sannio—weighted down by pearls and vessels of gold—is escorted to the surface by a squadron of nymphs.

Aside from the obvious structural parallels with the cosmography of the Dantesque *Paradise,* there is another more probable source for the general framework of Cueva's poem. Robert H. Williams has established that the model is the first dialogue of the *Dialoghi piacevoli* by Niccolò Franco (Venice, 1539).[2] In this version, Sannio, guided by Virtue, approaches heaven and challenges the gods because he is denied entrance. Momus intercedes on his behalf, and he is able to converse with Jupiter, is granted several favors, and returns to earth. Admitting that the fifth book is original, Williams writes (p. 198) that Cueva "enlarged on the material so freely that the plagiarism might have gone undetected if the protagonist's name had been changed. The

primer libro, for example, contains an extensive digression inter-
polated at the outset of the flight through heavenly space. The
Italian author had merely made a few remarks about the moon
and satirized astrologers, whereas his imitator indulged in a
bird's-eye description of the earth in a manner vaguely reminis-
cent of Cicero's *Somnium Scipionis.* Its very nature suggests
another borrowing."

The story of Sannio's magical flight may be traced ultimately
to the Greek humorist Lucian, whose *Dialogues of the Dead* are
almost outrageously comical. Guerrieri Crocetti suggested
similarities between the subterranean vision and an analogous
episode in Sannazaro's *Arcadia*: the phantasmagoria of rivers
separating as the pilgrims approach, the portrayal of Betis
seated with his left side reclining on a huge stone urn from
which emanates a torrent of water, the volume of which increases
as the god shakes water from his dripping beard.[3]

In attempting to penetrate Cueva's intent in casting himself
as Sannio, one must first confront his understanding of the concept of "virtue." Guerrieri Crocetti begged the question when he
concluded that Cueva's apologetic intent was to portray Seville
"in all her artistic glory, her rôle as a Maecenas . . . and to stress
that the recompense vainly requested of the gods after such
hostility and disappointment on earth and in heaven, was to be
found in this bright corner of the world, the valley of the Betis."[4]
What makes *Sannio's Journey* important is the manner in which
Cueva resolves the conceptual dialectic which germinated in
the subsoil of his earliest works and soon pervaded every facet
of his life. His poem is the affirmation of a literary ideology, the
virtue which he refuses to relinquish. The replies of Sannio to
the catechism in poetics accentuate Cueva's abiding faith in
mimesis, the discipline of artistic imitation. He insists that the
poet's only critique be his own conscience, and Cueva's dictated
an art carefully conceived, of heroic dignity expounded within
a historico-legendary framework.

II   Inventores de las cosas (The Inventors of Things)

The Inventors of Things is a treatise in blank verse divided
into four books of 798, 536, 542, and 411 lines, respectively. It

appears in two manuscripts and was published once, in the eighteenth century.[5] The poem is patterned on Polydorus Virgilius' *De rerum inventoribus* (Venice, 1499). An enormously popular work, the original three books were expanded to eight in a later edition (Basel, 1521).

In the dedicatory epistle to Doña Gerónima María de Guzmán (signed in Cuenca on May 9, 1607), Cueva establishes the lines of departure from a more immediate model, a Spanish translation of Polydorus by Vicente de Millis Godínez (Medina del Campo, 1599).[6] He claims that although requested to complete his version on short notice, it is by no means a slavish translation. Rather, he has "altered the organization, collated both Latin and Italian texts, and drawn from a variety of histories and dictionaries to emend obvious errors."

A curious compendium not without interest, the *Inventors* examines the most fundamental of human preoccupations and resources from the dawn of civilization. It reflects an understandable historico-legendary *sic et non,* the near impossible task of sifting myth and fact. López Sedano found that its merit resides in Cueva's fluid versification, which he called "generally harmonious and pleasant to the ear." On the other hand, he failed to perceive any method, chronology, or classification in the structure of this version, concluding that Cueva appears to have listed the inventors as they occurred to him. It must be admitted that Cueva's difficulty in reducing so vast a canvas to workable proportions is apparent. At the same time, he tends to single out progressive phases in mankind's search for knowledge. Within the greater historical context, Cueva lists the specific accomplishments of races, countries and dynasties, etc.

Book One begins with the legendary attribution of the fermentation of grape juice to Bacchus. Cueva elaborates on the ingenuity of this deity, crediting him with the discovery of blending wines and the invention of the cane. The author sometimes contradicts himself when he returns to the subject. For example, he declares that Bacchus taught man to prune the vines, but goes on to say that man learned the skill by first observing a donkey grazing on vine shoots. A characteristic of the *Inventors* is Cueva's insistence that many essential everyday customs and tools derive from the observation of natural phenomena: i.e., the saw suggested by the spiny backbone of the fish. Book One is devoted to the discovery and innovations in the basic sciences: agriculture, weaving, metallurgy, ceramics, carpentry, building, etc. In Book Two Cueva becomes more contemporary, discussing the practices and contributions of the Greeks and Romans—music and musical instruments, augury, sacrifices, astrology, timekeeping, games. Particular emphasis falls on literature and the fine arts. Cueva alludes to the famous Humanist of Seville, Fernando Colón, whose library of twenty thousand volumes formed the core of the Biblioteca Colombina.

Book Three brings the reader much closer to the present and acquaints him with the inventors of what Cueva terms the "diabolical devices"—artillery, gunpowder, dice and cards (the latter ascribed to a Catalan), and taxes! The final book—although much more general in coverage—does stress inventions and customs native to Seville. Cueva alludes to the four infamous refuges in his city where criminals could formerly find shelter from the law. Of particular interest is his description of the dragon figures (tarascas) seen in Seville during Corpus Christi celebrations, "so enormous that they tower over two-story buildings." The work ends with the amusing observation that the famous Roman general Scipio Africanus was the first to use aftershave lotions, "a practice criticized by those who did not understand the mystery."

The reaction of Doña Gerónima to Cueva's continuation of Polydorus is not known. It has been suggested that his contemporary, Cervantes, disparaged—if not the Sevillian's work—the whole lot of similar compilations which for him embodied pointless erudition for its own sake. The Supplement to Polydorus being prepared by his character—known only as the cousin (Quijote, II, Ch. 22)—is roundly ridiculed for having lost sight of the premises upon which meaningful humanistic investigation should be based. It is far from certain that Cueva was the intended recipient of Cervantes' barb. Cueva's continuation was not published during Cervantes' lifetime, and it is unlikely that the manuscript circulated widely. Even before it was completed, the Italian Vincenzo Bruno published his version, the Teatro degl' inventori di tutte le cose (Naples, 1603), which may well have caught Cervantes' critical eye.[7]

III *Unpublished Translations*

A. *The* Batalla entre ranas y ratones (Battle of the Frogs and Rats) *and the* Muracinda (Cat and Dog Fight)

The *Battle of the Frogs and Rats* is a burlesque poem patterned on the *Batracomyomachia* which is sometimes attributed to Homer. A parody of Homer's *Iliad*, the poem was translated into Latin in the sixteenth century by the Italian printer Aldo Manucio, whose version may have been used by Cueva. His translation is incomplete and appears only in a short fragment at the end of the Colombina MS. 82-2-5.

The *Cat and Dog Fight* is even more fragmentary, and the source has never been established. Both translations are from an indeterminate time and may be products of Cueva's old age as indicated by their position in the manuscript, or they may be from that period of his youth when—as Girón mentions— Cueva was engrossed in reading and translating Latin writers.

B. *Lost Works*

In addition to the missing second volume of plays, there are several other lacunae in Cueva's *opus*. He boasts in *Sannio's Journey* of having translated Martial, Horace, Juvenal, Tibullus, and Propertius. He also says—in words placed in Sannio's mouth —that he had written more short stories than Boccaccio. There is no evidence with which to substantiate any of these claims. Finally, Gallardo describes a manuscript, largely autograph, of Cueva's translation of the *Officina de Juan Ravisio Textor* dated 1582.[8] The manuscript has been missing since Gallardo saw it in Cadiz in 1844. A French Renaissance writer, Ravisius Textor describes the pedigrees of the pagan gods and their cults. This work was very popular in Spain.[9] He was also the author of a coarse farce entitled *Thersites* (*ca.* 1537) based on the character Audacious, the comic braggart soldier in Homer's *Iliad*.[10] It is possible that Cueva's version of the braggart soldier is partially imitated from Textor's.

CHAPTER 10

Cueva and the Critics

THE preceding chapters have shown that Juan de la Cueva is a difficult figure to approach. During his lifetime, those who knew him were able to form a true estimate of his literary accomplishments of the first magnitude. The value of humanistic learning was universally acknowledged and—despite Cueva's occasional recklessness—his formalism was highly regarded. That his posthumous fame was soon eclipsed is due, no doubt, to the very scant dissemination of his works. As time went on, Cueva lost even more ground. Within fifty years of his death, he was nearly forgotten in Spain and hardly appreciated outside it. For the next two centuries, references to Cueva would be limited to the often questionable cataloguing of his works by indifferent historians of literature. Predictably, their usually unfavorable evaluations were the result of imposing on Cueva's works the norms of current literary trends which ignored the spirit in which they were composed. Cueva's works are only now emerging from an unnecessarily long probation period to gain world currency. Promising new directions in literary criticism are permitting the message of the author to be heard in his own tongue. A brief summary of the long-prevailing attitudes toward Cueva's works will enable the reader to comprehend more fully the pendular movement that this criticism has followed.

The serious prefatory remarks of Maestro Diego Girón to Cueva's *Works*[1] enthusiastically herald the author's achievements and, at the same time, disarm possible detractors hostile to the classical modes:

His style is entirely fluid and smooth; it is uniform for the most part, although, here and there it crests in forceful emotion and tragic sublimity, since—as Latin writers knew—unpretentious subjects contain the seeds of tragic sentiment. The movement—which the ancients called the thread of the plot—is regular and linear. The

148

language is fitting, eloquent and pure since it is not adulterated by a mixture of affected neologisms drawn from other languages; the author was always respectful of his own language and he refused to imitate his contemporaries or their use of exaggerated metaphors, a practice only too prevalent among others. In short, in the author one finds that fluency and ease which Seneca rightly praised in Ovid, a writer greatly admired by our poet since his youth. From the very beginning, his aim in writing these verses was none other than his own entertainment and the satisfaction of knowing that this medium more so than any other captivated his imagination. But once he discovered that his poetic genius was greater than he himself would have thought, and at the request of friends whose judgment he respected, he decided to publish a sampling of his works as evidence of what could be expected of his intellect henceforth, for which his country also would be the better.

Recognition and praise are ephemeral qualities, and the anathema pronounced against Sannio by the god of ridicule was waiting to be fulfilled. Fame, so urgently sought by the author, would be meted out only in grudging measure. Years later, when Rodrigo Caro published his famous biography, *Varones insignes en letras naturales ... de Sevilla ... (Seville's Distinguished Men of Letters ...)* only the sparsest information on Cueva's works was included.[2] The Sevillian canon, Nicolás Antonio, overlooked all but a few of Cueva's published works. His enormously important *Biblioteca hispana nova (Catalogue of Recent Spanish Works)*—covering the years from 1500 to 1670—lists only the 1588 edition of the tragedies and comedies, the *Works* of 1582, the *Phoebean Chorus,* and the *Conquest of Andalusia.*[3]

It was inevitable that eventually Cueva's tragedies would provide grist for the mills of eighteenth-century academic debates over the national drama and its licitness. The lines were drawn between the neoclassicists and the nationalists who fought out their conceptual battles in the theatres which were dominated by translations or adaptations of French plays. Among the most outspoken Gallicists belonging to the prestigious Academy of Good Taste (Academia del Buen Gusto) were Ignacio de Luzán and Agustín de Montiano y Luyando. Both were consistently severe in condemning the Spanish national drama for its lack of classical formalism. The latter singles out Cueva for mild rebuke in his *Discurso sobre las tragedias españolas (Discourse on Span-*

ish Tragedies).[4] He objects to the title of the *Seven Infantes of Lara* because they do not appear in the play, and criticizes the disregard for the unities. He is positive only in his praise of the diction of the play. Concerning the *Tragedy of Ajax Telamon's Death*, he finds verisimilitude only in the portrayal of the two rivals. In the *Death of Virginia and Appius Claudius*, he criticizes the separable extraneous action—the trial and death of Claudius in the last act. The two-part *Tyrant Prince* he finds acceptable for its unity but censures it for unrealistic action. His comments are typical of the attitudes of this generation of writers toward Cueva's dramaturgy. Leandro Fernández de Moratín bases his comments in his *Orígenes del teatro español* (*Origins of the Spanish Drama*) on these and similar opinions.[5]

Not all Cueva's eighteenth-century commentators took exception to his importance. In fact, at about the same time as his tragedies were being picked apart, his heroic poem, *The Conquest of Andalusia* found strong defending voices abroad. In England, Hugh Blair praised the choice of subject matter in his *Lectures on Rhetoric and Belles Lettres* (London, 1783), but was somewhat less complimentary concerning its execution.

Among the Jesuits expelled from Spain in 1767 was Francisco Xavier Llampillas, who fled to Italy. There his patriotic sentiments led him to defend Spanish literary accomplishments against the fanatical attacks of such Italian chauvinists as Tiraboschi and Bettinelli. His defense and their responses were published in the *Saggio storico-apologetico della letteratura spagnuola* ... (*Historico-Apologetic Treatise on Spanish Literature* ...).[6] This work is particularly interesting because of Llampillas' evaluation of Cueva's epic poem and other works. He first addresses himself to the task of correcting Montiano's "misconceptions" about the tragedies. He finds precedents in Greek drama which justify all the liberties taken by the playwright. As for the *Conquest of Andalusia*, Llampillas states in a rapture of enthusiasm: "the lack of poetic innovation, for which Cueva has been criticized, is more than offset by the infinite number of exquisitely rhymed verses, sublime conceits, and a structure so well executed that it earned for him a place among the foremost epic poets of his day."

A contemporary of the apologist, Juan Joseph López de

Sedano, himself a writer of tragedy, was the greatest promul-
gator of Cueva's works during the eighteenth century. His verse
anthology in nine volumes—cited in preceding chapters—made
available many rare texts upon which he comments in prefatory
remarks.[7] Having selected an eclogue, three *canciones,* an elegy,
the *Poets' Guide,* and *The Inventors of Things* as representative
works, he defends Cueva's genius, urging that he be afforded his
rightful place in the annals of Spanish literary history. Writing
more specifically about the eclogue, he observes:

It is one of the best of all the lyric poems of this celebrated tragedian,
and should be appreciated for all of its qualities, namely, decorum
of the speakers, aptness of subject, sublimity and purity of verse,
and the abundant and graceful imitations of classical models.[8]

In the early nineteenth century, another ardent nationalist—
this one very actively opposed to French influences—found
Cueva's works intriguing. Manuel José Quintana included two
long excerpts from the *Conquest of Andalusia* in his great poetic
anthology.[9] Unfortunately, because of the superficial nature of
his analysis of the entire poem, his comments tend to be exces-
sively negative.[10] It is worth noting that his highly aspersive
criticism is strikingly similar to the wording of a preface to the
only posthumous printing of the poem—an edition by Pedro
Estala who used the pseudonym Ramón Fernández, which he
took from the name of his barber.[11] Volumes XIV and XV which
contain the poem—and the critical summary—were published
in 1795 by an anonymous editor after Estala's death. It has been
suggested that these remarks are really an abridged version of
Quintana's opinions of Cueva's poem.[12]

The nineteenth-century transition from Classicism to Romanticism is reflected in contradictory critical views of Cueva. Again
the drama is the area for much of the conceptual polemic, and
Cueva's production is once more under fire. In his own plays,
Francisco Martínez de la Rosa was one of the first of his generation to compromise on the question of formalism in the drama.
Yet the same ideas which governed the formulation of his literary theories—published in a *Poetics* and *Appendix on the Spanish
Tragedy*—color his appraisal of Cueva.[13] It disturbed him that
the Sevillian "failed to use models" and that his plots were "taken

largely from his imagination." He admits that Cueva contributed to the progress of Spanish tragedy, but accuses him of having led it astray by sanctioning freedom from classical forms. He was particularly incensed that Cueva should have attempted to promulgate his disdain for the rules in the *Poets' Guide,* for which he labels the author "all the more pernicious."

Less severe is the disenchantment of another Sevillian, Alberto Lista, who published his formal literary precepts in 1836.[14] His opinions are generally representative of the so-called School of Seville in the period of transition from Classicism to Romanticism. In large part, his observations are a summation of the clichés repeated for the preceding two hundred years. He credits Cueva with introducing polymetry to the drama, with being the first to utilize ballad fragments and historical themes. He does not dispute the claim that Cueva was the first to bring kings and noblemen to the stage as well as to dramatize sieges and assaults on cities. He attempts to show that Cueva borrowed from Torres Naharro much of his novelesque material which, according to Lista, he was unable to exploit satisfactorily.

The German poet and critic Adolf Friedrick von Schack discovered Cueva around the middle of the century. Generally, he repeats the judgments of Moratín and Lista, considering Cueva an essential force in the development of the national theatre.[15] His comments have colored subsequent criticism by hispanists in Germany.

Cueva's prestige again made an advance when Menéndez Pelayo called attention to his importance in contributing to the development and spread in Mexico of the good literary practices disseminated by the School of Seville.[16] This perspicacious critic saw Cueva's dramaturgy as a direct stimulus of the Spanish national theatre.[17] Likewise, Ludwig Pfandl promoted Cueva's rôle as precursor, and heralded especially his humanist erudition: "His fiery involvement in literary theorizing and polemics make him an author of great importance for the study of the metrics and precepts of his time."[18]

It is unfortunate that, in most recent times, consideration of Cueva has centered especially on the question of his influence in shaping the mature drama of Lope de Vega. Ramón Pérez de Ayala contends in his rather biased study of the drama, playwrights, and dramatic theory that formal precepts are always a consequence of practice and, hence, Cueva's dramatic theory is not the blossom without which the fruit would not have matured.[19] He concludes that in Cueva one finds "the essential traits of the national theatre already hearty and on the point of reaching the definitive form which they would assume in the agile hands of Lope. And these qualities are characteristic not just of Cueva and Lope, but of the Spanish people" (p. 96).

Even those who have labored to bring Cueva out of relative obscurity have, on occasion, made startling and sometimes inadmissable statements about his achievements. Icaza insists that the plays hold little interest for the modern reader and sees their value only as evidence of the transition within the genre at a particular historical moment.[20] It is just as difficult to accept Hermenegildo's contention that Cueva was a man of limited cultural resources with a weak humanistic background.[21] Marcel Bataillon unconvincingly argues that because Cueva took the precaution of publishing his plays, he automatically insured for himself a position of greater importance in history than he would have been afforded otherwise by his contemporaries.[22] This unsound argument is basic to several recent studies on the origins of the Spanish drama. Othón Arróniz, for example, looks beyond Cueva to Italian models in his search for the answer.[23] Likewise, Rinaldo Froldi's thesis that the seeds of the seventeenth-century *comedia* sprouted in the hands of the Valencian school of dramatists disregards Cueva as a formative influence.[24]

It should be obvious from the sampling of diverse views offered here that literary historians are not likely to find any time soon an exit from the maze of controversy while persisting in the timeworn "influences" approach to literature. This survey of Cueva's life and works has attempted to provide the basis for a more positive approach. Hopefully, it has shown a composite view of the intellectual basis which enriched the author and molded his art, and has placed the more fundamental questions in their proper perspective. But this is only a start. Students of Juan de la Cueva henceforth must develop empirical analytical methods with which to approach the wealth of original material bequeathed by the author to posterity. Literary history can never transcend a sterile cataloguing of facts unless the student is willing to examine the texts himself and discover the mysteries of the creative imagination. Those who make this effort are sure to derive often unsuspected satisfaction from the hidden treasures of Juan de la Cueva.

Notes and References

Chapter One

1. "Poèmes inédits de Juan de la Cueva," *Lunds Universitets Arsskrift,* XXIII (1887), i-c, 1-64.

2. The latter appears in several MSS: No. 82-2-5 of the Biblioteca Colombina, and MS. 4.116 of the Biblioteca Nacional. It was published in *Archivo Hispalense,* I (1886), 261-72, 290-309.

3. These details from the *History* are included in the study by Camillo Guerrieri Crocetti, *Juan de la Cueva e le origini del teatro nazionale spagnuolo* (Turin: Gambino, 1936), p. 10.

4. Included among the prefatory remarks of his *Parnaso español. Colección de poesías escogidas de los más célebres poetas castellanos,* 9 vols. (Madrid: Antonio de Sancha, 1768-1778), VIII (1774), xv.

5. Guerrieri Crocetti, p. 17.

6. *Sucesos reales que parecen imaginados, de Gutierre de Cetina, Juan de la Cueva y Mateo Alemán* (Madrid: Fortanet, 1919), pp. 88-89.

7. The careers of Cueva's cousins are discussed by Wulff, pp. xxxv-xxxvi, and by Icaza, pp. 83-87.

8. Edwin S. Morby, "The Plays of Juan de la Cueva," unpublished doctoral dissertation, University of California (Berkeley, 1936), p. 48.

9. Wulff, pp. xli-xlv.

10. *Juan de la Cueva . . . ,* pp. 25-26.

11. Printed in part by Wulff, pp. xliv-xlv.

12. Pages xxxvii-xlvii of Wulff's study refer to this epoch of Cueva's life.

13. Printed by Wulff, p. xliii.

14. "Poèmes inédits . . . ," lvii-lviii.

15. *Fernando de Herrera (el Divino) 1534-1597* (Paris: Champion, 1908), p. 75.

16. A fragment of this epistle was included by Bartolomé José Gallardo y Blanco in his *Ensayo de una biblioteca española de libros raros y curiosos,* 4 vols. (Madrid: Rivadeneyra, 1863-1869), II (1866), cols. 647-48. The only epistle by Cueva to be published in its entirety in modern times, it was edited by Higinio Capote Porrúa in *Anuario de Estudios Americanos,* IX (1952), 597-616.

155

17. *Sucesos reales* . . . , pp. 113-14.

18. He argues for Cueva as the probable compiler in two articles: *"Flores de baria poesía*: Apuntes preliminares para el estudio de un cancionero mexicano del siglo XVI," *Hispania*, XXXIV (1951), 177-80; and *"Flores de baria poesía*. Estudio preliminar de un *Cancionero* inédito mexicano de 1577," *Ábside*, XV (1951), 373-96, 523-50.

19. *"Flores de baria poesía" Un cancionero inédito mexicano de 1577*, ed. Renato Rosaldo (Mexico: Ábside, 1952). This edition is based on a copy of the original manuscript—No. 2973 of the Biblioteca Nacional—which was made by Antonia Paz y Melia because of the serious deterioration of the autograph.

20. *Romances of Chivalry in the Spanish Indies* (Berkeley: University of California Press, 1933), p. 15.

21. Wulff, p. li.

22. Wulff, p. lii.

23. Cited by Marcel N. Schveitzer, *Spain* (Paris: Hachette, 1961), pp. 736-37.

24. Guerrieri Crocetti, p. 22.

25. *Ibid.*, pp. 14-15.

26. Adolphe Coster, *Fernando de Herrera* . . . , pp. 19-20.

27. *Ibid.*, p. 22.

28. Cited by Coster, p. 23.

29. "The Academies and Seventeenth-Century Spanish Literature," *Publications of the Modern Language Association of America*, LXXV (1960), 367-76. While Professor King writes more specifically of the seventeenth-century academies, her conclusions are nonetheless true for the antecedents.

30. The complex geneology of this family was painstakingly traced by Wulff, pp. lxii-lxiii.

31. See Francisco M. Tubino, *Pablo de Céspedes* (Madrid, 1868).

32. Francisco Rodríguez Marín, *Luis Barahona de Soto. Estudio biográfico, bibliográfico y crítico* (Madrid: Sucesores de Rivadeneyra, 1903), p. 149, n. 2.

33. José Sánchez, *Academias literarias del siglo de oro español* (Madrid: Gredos, 1961), p. 207.

34. Wulff, pp. lviii-lxv.

35. Gallardo, cols. 674-75.

36. Coster, pp. 75-76.

37. *Loc. cit.*

38. The only available biographical data relevant to Medina is that provided by Pacheco in the eulogy of the man in his *Libro de* . . . *retratos* . . . , which is summarized by Coster, pp. 27-31.

39. Coster, p. 107.

40. Sánchez, *Academias literarias . . .* , p. 199.

41. Coster, pp. 120-21.

42. *Ibid.,* pp. 115-16.

43. *Ibid.,* pp. 79-81.

Chapter Two

1. N. D. Shergold, *A History of the Spanish Stage from Medieval Times until the End of the Seventeenth Century* (Oxford: Clarendon, 1967), p. 451.

2. Cited by Joaquín Hazañas y la Rúa, *Obras de Gutierre de Cetina,* 2 vols. (Madrid: P. Díaz, 1895), I, xc.

3. José Sánchez Arjona, *El teatro en Sevilla en los siglos XVI y XVII* (Madrid: Alonso, 1887), p. 204.

4. Federico Sánchez Escribano attributes the play to Mal Lara in his study, *Juan de Mal Lara. Su vida y sus obras* (New York: Hispanic Institute, 1941), pp. 166-68.

5. J. P. Wickersham Crawford, *Spanish Drama before Lope de Vega* (Philadelphia: University of Pennsylvania Press, 1922), p. 157.

6. The survey by J. García Soriano ["El teatro escolar en España," *Boletín de la Real Academia Española,* XIV (1927), XV (1928), XVI (1929), XIX (1932)] is incomplete.

7. Shergold, p. 173.

8. Adolfo Bonilla y San Martín, "El teatro escolar en el renacimiento español y un fragmento inédito del toledano Juan Pérez," *Homenaje ofrecido a Menéndez Pidal,* 3 vols. (Madrid: Hernando, 1925), III, 143-55.

9. *Los trágicos españoles del siglo XVI* (Madrid: Raycar, 1961).

10. Crawford, pp. 162-64.

11. *Ibid.,* p. 176.

12. "The Influence of Senecan Tragedy in the Plays of Juan de la Cueva," *Studies in Philology,* XXXIV (1937), 383-91. This article is a condensation of his findings in "The Plays of Juan de la Cueva," unpublished doctoral dissertation, University of California (Berkeley, 1936).

13. Morby, "The Plays . . . ," p. 36.

14. *Ibid.,* p. 32.

15. *The Influence of Plautus in Spain before Lope de Vega* (Lancaster, Pa.: Lancaster Press, 1944), pp. 168-69.

16. "Romance a la musa Talía," in the unpublished MS. of the *Coro febeo de romances historiales* (Biblioteca Colombina MS. 82-2-5 *bis*).

17. S. Griswold Morley, "Strophes in the Spanish Drama before Lope de Vega," *Homenaje ofrecido a Menéndez Pidal,* 3 vols. (Madrid: Hernando, 1925), I, 505-31.

18. "The Plays . . . ," p. 21.

19. Morby, *op. cit.,* p. 22.

20. *Ibid.,* pp. 21-30.

21. For an account of Lope's debt to these influences, see Richard F. Glenn, "The Impact of the Spanish Pastoral Romance on Lope de Vega's Dramatic Art," *Annali,* XIII (1971), 5-25.

22. Guerrieri Crocetti, *Juan de la Cueva . . . ,* especially the concluding chapter.

23. "Juan de la Cueva y el drama histórico," *Nueva Revista de Filología Hispánica,* IX (1955), 152.

24. "Dramatic Unity in the Plays of Juan de la Cueva," unpublished doctoral dissertation, Duke University (Durham, North Carolina, 1970).

25. *Juan de la Cueva and the Portuguese Succession* (London: Tamesis, 1971).

26. Ronald Boal Williams, *The Staging of Plays in the Spanish Peninsula Prior to 1555,* The University of Iowa Studies in Spanish Language and Literature, No. 5 (Iowa City, 1935).

27. Shergold, pp. 110-11.

28. *Ibid.,* pp. 158-67.

29. Shergold, "Ganassa and the *Commedia dell'arte* in Sixteenth-Century Spain," *Modern Language Review,* LI (1956), 359-68.

30. Othón Arróniz, *La influencia italiana en el nacimiento de la comedia española* (Madrid: Gredos, 1969), p. 209.

31. Sánchez Arjona, pp. 87-88.

32. *Ibid.,* p. 47.

33. The résumé of the stage description is taken from the article by N. D. Shergold, "Juan de la Cueva and the Early Theatres of Seville," *Bulletin of Hispanic Studies,* XXXII (1955), 1-7.

Chapter Three

1. See Ramón Menéndez Pidal, *La leyenda de los Infantes de Lara* (Madrid: Ducazal, 1896), pp. 121-26.

2. Cited by Menéndez Pidal, *loc. cit.*

3. Appearing in two manuscripts (MS. 82-2-5 of the Biblioteca Colombina and MS. 4.116 of the Biblioteca Nacional), this eclogue was published by Gallardo, *Ensayo . . . ,* II, cols. 720-23.

4. For a survey of Spanish literature treating this ideology, see Harry Austin Deferrari, *The Sentimental Moor in Spanish Literature before 1600* (Philadelphia: University of Pennsylvania Press, 1927).

5. See E. H. Templin, *The Exculpation of "Yerros por Amores" in the Spanish Comedia* (Berkeley: University of California Press, 1933).

6. Anthony Watson, pp. 64-80.

7. Bruce W. Wardropper has argued that this antithesis is the basis for Lope de Vega's most perfect play: "*Fuente Ovejuna: El gusto* and *lo justo*," *Studies in Philology*, III (1956), 159-71.

8. *L'Epopée castillane à travers la littérature espagnole*, tr. Henri Mérimée (Paris: Armand Colin, 1910).

9. *El cantar de Sancho II y cerco de Zamora* (Madrid: *Revista de Filología Española* [Anejo XXXVII], 1947). Pp. 159-62 refer specifically to Cueva's play.

10. *Cantar de gesta de Don Sancho II de Castilla* (Madrid: Fortanet, 1911).

11. Pp. 36-51.

12. The *suelta*, owned by the Hispanic Society of America, has been described by J. P. Wickersham Crawford, "The 1603 Edition of Cueva's *Comedia del saco de Roma*," *Modern Language Notes*, XLIV (1929), 389. He reports that the text follows closely the edition of 1583.

13. The best recent survey of the situation is to be found in the chapter by Professor H. Koenigsberger in *The New Cambridge Modern History*, 14 vols. (Cambridge: Cambridge University Press, 1957-), II (1958), 301-33.

14. J. P. Wickersham Crawford, *Spanish Drama . . .*, p. 168.

15. P. 177.

16. Edwin S. Morby, "The Plays . . . ," p. 105.

17. *Ibid.*

18. Pp. 52-63.

19. The historical background of Cueva's play is covered by Guerrieri Crocetti in Ch. 6, pp. 123-39.

20. The recurrence of the epic material in the drama has been traced by Richard Mitterer in *Die Saga von Bernardo del Carpio im spanischen Drama des XVI und XVII Jahrhunderts* (Würzburg: G. Grasser, 1930).

21. The significance of this concept for subsequent Spanish literature is discussed in a brilliant study by Leo Spitzer, "Classical and Christian Ideas of World Harmony: Prolegomena to an Interpretation of the Word *Stimmung*," *Traditio*, II (1944), 409-64.

22. Watson, pp. 81-99.

Chapter Four

1. Ajax' death had been dramatized by Sophocles in the fifth century and by Seneca in his *Troades*, but never before rendered in Spanish.

2. Gilbert Highet, *The Classical Tradition, Greek and Roman*

Influences on Western Literature (New York: Oxford University Press, 1949), p. 273.

3. Icaza, *Sucesos reales* . . . , p. 144.

4. Watson, pp. 100-117.

5. Icaza, p. 145. Ovid's account in Book XIII of the *Metamorphoses* seems more remote. Livy, Book III, is the probable source.

6. MS. 82-2-5 *bis* of the Biblioteca Colombina. Morby confuses this MS. with another, No. 4.070 of the Biblioteca Nacional.

7. Helmut Petriconi, "El tema de Lucrecia y Virginia," *Clavileño*, II (1951), 1-5.

8. Morby, "The Plays . . . , p. 114.

9. Icaza, p. 146.

10. Alfredo Hermenegildo, pp. 312-13.

11. Moratín, Schack, Icaza, and others share this view.

12. Grismer, pp. 24-25.

13. Watson, pp. 151-61.

Chapter Five

1. *Origenes del teatro español*, in *Biblioteca de Autores Españoles*, II (Madrid: Rivadeneyra, 1930), p. 212.

2. Professor Joseph E. Gillet investigates the degree of promulgation of this theory in his article, "Cueva's *Comedia del Infamador* and the Don Juan Legend," *Modern Language Notes*, XXXVII (1922), 206-12. He claims that Alberto Lista was the probable originator of this interpretation in his *Lecciones de literatura española* (Madrid, 1836).

3. Icaza, *Comedias y tragedias de Juan de la Cueva*, I, xlviii-xlix. Gillet, see above. Valbuena, *Historia de la literatura española*, 8th ed., rev., 4 vols. (Barcelona: Gustavo Gili, 1968), I, 835.

4. *Spanish Drama* . . . , p. 169.

5. The genesis of this motif as it appears in Tirso's play has been established by Professor Gerald E. Wade in the Introduction to his excellent edition of the work (New York: Scribners, 1969).

6. Literary continuations of the type are traced by María Rosa Lida de Malkiel, *La originalidad artística de La Celestina* (Buenos Aires: Editorial Universitaria, 1962), pp. 573 and 714-16.

7. For a useful discussion of the appearance of this character in the early Spanish drama, see J. P. Wickersham Crawford, "The Braggart Soldier and the *Rufián* in the Spanish Drama of the Sixteenth Century," *Romanic Review*, II (1911), 186-208.

8. Watson, pp. 181-99.

9. Pp. 162-80.

10. Crawford (*Spanish Drama* . . . , p. 169) observes that Giraldi

Cinthio's fifth story of the eighth Decade of *Gli Hecatommithi* or his dramatization of the story, entitled *Epitia,* are the probable sources of Cueva's play.

11. "The Plays . . . ," p. 131.

12. Icaza, p. xlv and Valbueba Prat, I, 834.

13. "Dramatic Unity . . . ," pp. 106-33.

14. "The Plays . . . ," p. 136

15. *Ibid.,* p. 140.

Chapter Six

1. The sonnet was printed by Gallardo, *Ensayo* . . . , II, col. 688.

2. It can be read in MS. 82-2-5 of the Biblioteca Colombina, MS. 4.116 of the Biblioteca Nacional, and the Gor manuscript, described by Walberg.

3. "Le poème *Llanto de Venus en la muerte de Adonis* de Juan de la Cueva dans sa version définitive en partie inédite," *Mélanges offerts à Marcel Bataillon* (Bordeaux: Féret et Fils, 1962), pp. 677-89.

4. Otis H. Green, *"Fingen los poetas*: Notes on the Spanish Attitude toward Pagan Mythology," *Estudios dedicados a Don Ramón Menéndez Pidal,* 8 vols. (Madrid: Consejo Superior de Investigaciones Científicas, 1950), I, 275-88.

5. "Poèmes inédits . . . ," xxi.

6. *Biblioteca de Autores Españoles,* LXV (Madrid: Hernando, 1929), 453-60.

7. Marcelino Menéndez Pelayo, *Horacio en España,* 2 vols. (Madrid: Pérez Dubrull, 1885), II, 49.

8. *Ibid.,* 53.

9. Reprinted by Gallardo, II, col. 647.

10. "La epístola quinta de Juan de la Cueva," *Anuario de Estudios Americanos,* IX (1952), 615.

11. Salazar lived in Mexico from 1581 to 1589. His epistle was published by Gallardo, IV, col. 3776.

12. Menédez Pelayo, pp. 54-55.

13. *Spain and the Western Tradition,* 4 vols. (Madison: University of Wisconsin Press, 1968), I, 213-15.

14. *Estudios sobre el petrarquismo en España* (Madrid: *Revista de Filología Española* [Anejo LXXII], 1960), p. 91.

15. The contents of the manuscript (No. 82-2-4 of the Biblioteca Colombina) are described by Gallardo, II, cols. 654-716.

16. "De las rimas de Juan de la Cueva, Primera Parte," *Homenaje a Menéndez y Pelayo,* 2 vols. (Madrid: Suárez, 1899), II, 143-48.

17. MS. 82-2-5 of the Biblioteca Colombina.

Chapter Seven

1. Tasso's poem was translated into Spanish almost immediately by Bartolomé Cayrasco de Figueroa in 1585 and by Juan Sedeño in 1587.

2. Using the pen name Ramón Fernández, the anonymous editor —probably Manuel José Quintana—wrote in 1795, "There are still some readers today who enjoy the *autos* of Calderón and Gracián's prose, and the *Conquest* is superior to either of these" (*Colección de poesías castellanas . . .*, XIV, 15).

3. *Ibid.*, p. 13.

4. Arturo Farinelli, *Italia e Spagna*, 2 vols. (Turin: Fratelli Bocca, 1929), II, 245.

5. Francis William Pierce, *La poesía épica del siglo de oro* (Madrid: Gredos, 1961), p. 309.

6. *Colección de poesías castellanas . . .*, XIV, 9.

7. Ramón Menéndez Pidal, *El romancero español* (New York: Hispanic Society of America, 1910), pp. 74-75.

8. Gallardo (*Ensayo . . .*, II, cols. 726-32) describes the contents of a manuscript now found in the Biblioteca Colombina (No. 82-2-5 *bis*) which is not in Cueva's handwriting. It contains eighty-nine ballads. A second manuscript, No. 4.070 of the Biblioteca Nacional, contains eighty-seven ballads, most of which were printed in the 1587 edition.

9. *Biblioteca de Autores Españoles*, X (1849) and XVI (1851).

10. *Orígenes de la novela*, 4 vols. (Madrid: Aldus, 1961), IV, 260.

11. "La antología griega en España," *Humanidades*, XXIV (1934), 11-15.

12. "The Plays . . . ," pp. 110-13.

13. *Ibid.*, p. 51.

14. *Fábulas mitológicas en España* (Madrid: Espasa-Calpe, 1952), pp. 11-15.

Chapter Eight

1. This controversy has been thoroughly investigated by Joaquín de Entrambasaguas in *Una guerra literaria del Siglo de Oro: Lope de Vega y los preceptistas aristotélicos* (Madrid: Tipografía de Archivos, 1932).

2. MS. 82-2-5 of the Biblioteca Colombina.

3. The later version can be read in MS. 10.182 of the Biblioteca Nacional which is an autograph and shows Cueva's corrections over mistaken readings.

4. *Parnaso español. Colección de poesías . . .*, VIII (1774), 1-68.

In his introduction, López describes the manuscript which he used as an autograph signed by Cueva and dated 1605, a date believed to be erroneous.

5. "Juan de la Cueva et son *Ejemplar poético,*" *Lunds Universitets Arsskrift,* XXXIX (1904), 1-113.

6. Walberg, p. 15.

7. R. R. Bolgar, *The Classical Heritage and its Beneficiaries* (Cambridge: Cambridge University Press, 1954), p. 529.

8. This and subsequent references to line numbers of each epistle refer to the numbering of the Walberg edition.

9. Adolphe Coster, *Fernando de Herrera . . .* , pp. 79-81.

10. Marcelino Menéndez Pelayo, *Antología de poetas líricos castellanos,* 10 vols. (Santander: Aldus, 1944-1945), X (1945), 148-50.

11. Walberg, pp. 31-33.

12. Guerrieri Crocetti, pp. 206-7.

13. Crawford, *Spanish Drama . . .* , pp. 94-96.

14. Walberg, p. 11.

15. Crawford, pp. 84-85.

16. Walberg, p. 12.

Chapter Nine

1. "Poèmes inédits . . . ," 1-62. He describes the manuscripts on pages iii-xxxiv, and includes a chapter on the language and versification, pp. lxxi-c.

2. "Francisco de Cáceres, Niccolò Franco and Juan de la Cueva," *Hispanic Review,* XXVII (1959), 194-99.

3. *Juan de la Cueva . . . ,*" pp. 50-51.

4. *Ibid.,* p. 45.

5. The work may be read in the Colombina MS. 82-2-5 and in MS. 10.182 of the Biblioteca Nacional; the only edition is that of López Sedano, *Parnaso español . . .* , IX (1778), 259-339.

6. Cited by López Sedano (xxxix of his Introduction). The first Spanish translation of the works of this Italian Humanist was that of Francisco Támara in 1550.

7. *Don Quijote de la Mancha,* ed. Francisco Rodríguez Marín, 10 vols. (Madrid: Ediciones Atlas, 1948), V, 152, n. 1.

8. *Ensayo . . .* , II, cols. 736-37.

9. Seventeenth-century interest in the work is discussed by Alan Trueblood, "The *Officina* of Ravisius Textor in Lope de Vega's *Dorotea,*" *Hispanic Review,* XXVI (1958), 135-41.

10. Gilbert Highet, *The Classical Tradition, Greek and Roman Influences on Western Literature,* pp. 137-38.

Chapter Ten

1. *Obras de Juan de la Cueva* . . . , fol. 5-7.

2. Ed. Santiago Montoto (Seville: Real Academia Sevillana de Buenas Letras, 1915), p. 66.

3. (Madrid, 1696), I, 682, cols. a, b.

4. (Madrid: Joseph de Orga, 1750), pp. 16-23.

5. *Biblioteca de Autores Españoles,* II (Madrid: Rivadeneyra, 1830), 210-16.

6. Tr. Josefa Amor y Borbón (Zaragoza, 1782), III, 83-89.

7. *Parnaso español* . . . , IV (1770), VIII (1774), and IX (1778) contain selections by Cueva.

8. IV (1770), xxviii.

9. *Poesías selectas castellanas . . . Segunda parte. Musa épica* (Madrid: D. M. de Burgos, 1833), V, 161-216.

10. A thorough survey of critical reaction to the poem is available in the study by Francis W. Pierce, *La poesía épica del siglo de oro,* 2nd ed. (Madrid: Gredos, 1968).

11. *Colección de poesías castellanas,* 15 vols. (Madrid: Imprenta Real, 1789-1795).

12. George Ticknor, *Historia de la literatura española,* tr. Pascual Gayangos y Arce, 2 vols. (Paris: Hachette, 1870), II, 39 n.

13. *Obras completas,* 4 vols. (Paris: Baudry, 1844-1845), I (1845), 66-67.

14. *Lecciones de literatura española esplicadas en el ateneo científico, literario y artístico* (Madrid: Nicolás Arias, 1836), pp. 107-14.

15. *Historia de la literatura y del arte dramático en España,* tr. Eduardo de Mier, 5 vols. (Madrid: M. Hello, 1885-87), I (1885), 430-46.

16. *Historia de la poesía hispano-americana,* 2 vols. (Madrid: Suárez, 1911), I, 33-35.

17. Marcelino Menéndez Pelayo, *Historia de las ideas estéticas en España,* 4th ed., rev., 9 vols. (Madrid: Hernando, 1929-1931), III (1930), 346-50.

18. *Historia de la literature nacional española en la edad de oro,* tr. Jorge Rubió Balaguer (Barcelona: Sucesores de Juan Gili, 1933), p. 122.

19. *Las máscaras,* 2 vols. (Madrid: Renacimiento, 1924), II, 91-97.

20. *Sucesos reales* . . . , pp. 153-54.

21. *Los trágicos españoles* . . . , p. 28.

22. "Simples réflexions sur Juan de la Cueva," *Bulletin Hispanique,* XXXVII (1935), 329-36.

23. *La influencia italiana en el nacimiento de la comedia española* (Madrid: Gredos, 1969).

24. *Lope de Vega y la formación de la comedia* (Salamanca: Anaya, 1968).

Selected Bibliography

PRIMARY SOURCES

Works by Juan de la Cueva

1. Dramatic Works:

CUEVA DE GAROZA, JUAN DE LA. *Primera parte de las comedias y tragedias de Juan de la Cueva dirigidas a Momo* (Seville: Andrea Pescioni, 1583). Contains the fourteen extant plays. The only known copy of this edition is in the Nationalbibliothek in Vienna.

————. *Primera parte de las comedias y tragedias de Juan de la Cueva dirigidas a Momo* (Seville: Juan de León, 1588). This second printing of the fourteen plays corrects errors and omissions in the earlier edition, and includes plot summaries and short synopses before each act. There are extant two copies in the Biblioteca Nacional and one in the British Museum.

————. *Comedia del saco de Roma* (Barcelona: Sebastián de Cormellas, 1603). A rare *suelta*, one of the few surviving from the late sixteenth-century theatre.

————. *Comedias y tragedias de Juan de la Cueva*, ed. Francisco A. de Icaza. 2 vols. (Madrid: Sociedad de Bibliófilos Españoles, 1917). Limited to only three hundred copies, this is the only complete modern edition of the plays. It lists no variants and is based entirely on the 1588 printing.

————. *El saco de Roma* and *El infamador*, ed. Eugenio de Ochoa. In *Tesoro del teatro español desde su orígen hasta nuestros días*, I (Paris: Baudry, 1838). A typical anthology edition.

————. *El infamador* and *Los siete Infantes de Lara*, ed. Francisco A. de Icaza (Madrid: Espasa-Calpe, 1924). The most easily accessible selection of these plays, it has been reprinted several times. Icaza's introduction is the same as that to his Bibliófilos edition.

————. *Comedia de la muerte del rey don Sancho*, ed. J. R. Lomba y Pedraja. In *Biblioteca Literaria del Estudiante*, XV (*Teatro anterior a Lope de Vega*) Madrid: Instituto Escuela, 1924. A standard school-text edition, abridged.

167

————. *Los siete Infantes de Lara,* ed. Carlos Sáinz de Robles. In *El teatro español: historia y antología,* I (Madrid: Aguilar, 1942). The 1588 text is modernized.

————. *Teatro escogido,* ed. Eduardo Fernández Marqués. In *Bibliotecas Populares Cervantes,* XCV (Madrid: Ibero-Americana de Publicaciones, n.d.). The standard school-text edition containing *El infamador* and *Los siete Infantes de Lara.*

————. *El infamador* and *Los siete Infantes de Lara,* ed. José Sánchez Fontáns (Buenos Aires: Espasa-Calpe [Colección Austral, 895], 1949). An accessible edition with a bibliography.

————. *El infamador,* ed. José Caso González (Salamanca: Anaya [Biblioteca Anaya, 65], 1965). A fine edition with a good introduction, text, and notes.

————. *El infamador,* ed. Everett W. Hesse and Juan O. Valencia. In *El teatro anterior a Lope de Vega* (Madrid: Alcalá, 1971). The most recent inclusion of Cueva's drama in a nonscholarly anthology.

2. Nondramatic Works:

Cueva de Garoza, Juan de la. *Conquista de la Bética* (Seville: Francisco Pérez, 1603). The princeps edition.

————. *Conquista de la Bética,* ed. Ramón Fernández. In *Colección de poesías castellanas,* XIV & XV (Madrid: Imprenta Real, 1795). The only complete posthumous edition.

————. *Coro febeo de romances historiales* (Seville: Juan de León, 1587). The only collection of Cueva's ballads published during his lifetime.

————. In *Romancero general,* ed. Agustín Durán. 2 vols. (Madrid: Rivadeneyra [Biblioteca de Autores Españoles, X & XVI], 1849, 1851). The most accessible anthology of many of Cueva's historical ballads.

————. *Ejemplar poético,* ed. Juan Joseph López de Sedano. In *Parnaso español. Colección de poesías escogidas de los más célebres poetas castellanos,* VIII (Madrid: Antonio de Sancha, 1774). The first edition of the work, based on a MS. now lost.

————. *Ejemplar poético,* ed. E. Walberg. In "Juan de la Cueva et son *Ejemplar poético,*" *Lunds Universitets Arsskrift,* XXXIX (1904), 1-113. Based on the MS. 82-2-5 of the Biblioteca Colombina, this is the most reliable edition and includes a substantial study of the work and of Cueva's poetics.

————. *Historia de la Cueva.* In *Archivo Hispalense,* I (1886), 261-72, 290-309. The only edition of the geneological poem.

————. *Inventores de las cosas*, ed. Juan Joseph López de Sedano. In *Parnaso español. Colección de poesías escogidas de los más célebres poetas castellanos*, IX (Madrid: Antonio de Sancha, 1778). The only printed version of the work.

————. *Obras de Juan de la Cueva dirigidas al ilustrísimo señor don Juan Téllez Girón....* (Seville: Andrea Pescioni, 1582). The author's collection of predominantly amatory verse.

————. *La poesía de Juan de la Cueva*, ed. E. Caldrea (Genoa: Bozzi, 1970). A limited edition already out of print.

SECONDARY SOURCES

1. Studies Devoted to Juan de la Cueva:

BARRET, LINTON I. "The Supernatural in Juan de la Cueva's Drama," *Studies in Philology*, XXXVI (1939), 147-68. An adequate study.

BATAILLON, MARCEL. "Simples réflexions sur Juan de la Cueva," *Bulletin Hispanique*, XXXVII (1935), 329-36. Reprinted as "Unas reflexiones sobre Juan de la Cueva," *Varia lección de clásicos españoles* (Madrid: Gredos, 1964). A thoughtful attempt to define Cueva's rôle in the formation of the *comedia*.

BATTLE, JOHN WAYNE. "Dramatic Unity in the Plays of Juan de la Cueva." Unpublished doctoral dissertation. Duke University (Durham, North Carolina, 1970). An imaginative appraisal of Cueva's dramas which elucidates their intrinsic value as works of art.

CAPOTE PORRÚA, HIGINIO. "La epístola quinta de Juan de la Cueva," *Anuario de Estudios Americanos*, IX (1952), 597-616. The only complete text of the epistle to Laurencio Sánchez de Obregón, printed in part by Gallardo.

CASO GONZÁLEZ JOSÉ. "*La muerte del rey don Sancho* de Juan de la Cueva y sus fuentes tradicionales," *Archivum*, XV (1965), 126-41. A cataloguing of Cueva's sources for this play.

CRAWFORD, J. P. WICKERSHAM. "A Sixteenth-Century Analogue of *Measure for Measure*," *Modern Language Notes*, XXXV (1920), 330-34. An interesting discussion of the parallels between the *Comedia del degollado* and Shakespeare's play.

————. "The 1603 Edition of Cueva's *Comedia del saco de Roma*," *Modern Language Notes*, XLIV (1929), 389. Describes the *suelta*, printed by Sebastián de Cormellas, in Barcelona.

GILLET, JOSEPH E. "Cueva's *Comedia del Infamador* and the Don Juan Legend," *Modern Language Notes*, XXXVII (1922), 206-12. An excellent résumé of critical judgments on Cueva's originality in creating the Don Juan type which concludes that the play, "considered as a whole, may be stated to contain an important preliminary sketch of the now traditional Don Juan."

GUERRIERI CROCETTI, CAMILLO. *Juan de la Cueva e le origini del teatro nazionale spagnuolo* (Turin: Gambino, 1936). An unconvincing study which finds in Cueva's historico-legendary plays the seeds of the seventeenth-century *comedia*.

HÄMEL, ADALBERT. *Der Cid im spanischen Drama des XVI und XVII Jahrhunderts* (Halle: Niemeyer, 1910). Traces dramatizations of the Cid including Cueva's play *The Death of King Sancho*.

––––––. "Juan de la Cueva und die Erstausgabe seiner *Comedias y Tragedias*," *Zeitschrift für Romanische Philologie*, XLIII (1923), 134-53. An article concerning the variants in the two printings of Cueva's dramas.

––––––. "Sobre la primera edición de las obras dramáticas de Juan de la Cueva," *Revista de Filología Española*, X (1923), 182-83. A shortened version of the previous article.

ICAZA, FRANCISCO A. DE. "Juan de la Cueva," *Boletín de la Real Academia Española*, IV (1917), 469-83, 612-26. Corrects misconceptions about Cueva in Julio Cejador's *History of Spanish Literature*.

MORBY, EDWIN S. "Notes on Juan de la Cueva: Versification and Dramatic Theory," *Hispanic Review*, VIII (1940), 213-18. Discusses Cueva's strophic variety and its application.

––––––. "The Influence of Senecan Tragedy in the Plays of Juan de la Cueva," *Studies in Philology*, XXXIV (1937), 383-91. An incisive article which illuminates the strong Senecan vein in Cueva's plays.

––––––. "The Plays of Juan de la Cueva." Unpublished doctoral dissertation. University of California (Berkeley, 1936). A basically sound study of Cueva's dramaturgy.

PFANDL, LUDWIG. "Studien zu Juan de la Cueva," *Archiv für das Studium der neueren Sprachen*, CLIX (1931), 231-53. Speculates on how the rare 1583 printing of the dramas reached the Vienna library.

ROSALDO, RENATO. "*Flores de baria poesía*: Apuntes preliminares para el estudio de un cancionero mexicano del siglo XVI," *Hispania*, XXXIV (1951), 177-80. See next entry.

––––––. "*Flores de baria poesía*. Estudio preliminar de un cancionero inédito mexicano de 1577," *Ábside*, XV (1951), 373-96, 523-50. Argues in favor of Cueva's compilation of the codex.

––––––. "*Flores de baria poesía*." *Un cancionero inédito mexicano de 1577*, ed. Renato Rosaldo (Mexico City: Ábside, 1952). An anthological study of the manuscript which includes six of Cueva's sonnets.

SHERGOLD, N. D. "Juan de la Cueva and the Early Theatres of Seville," *Bulletin of Hispanic Studies*, XXXII (1955), 1-7. Reprinted in Spanish as "Juan de la Cueva y los primeros teatros de Seville," *Archivo Hispalense*, No. 75 (1956), 57-64. The physical qualities of the stage are reconstructed from internal evidence in Cueva's plays.

SPERANDEO, G. "Some Aspects of Juan de la Cueva's Dramatic Art." Unpublished M.A. thesis. University of North Carolina (Chapel Hill, 1931). Of limited interest.

VERDEVOYE, PAUL. "Le poème *Llanto de Venus en la muerte de Adonis* de Juan de la Cueva dans sa version définitive en partie inédite," *Mélanges offerts à Marcel Bataillon* (Bordeaux: Féret et Fils, 1962), pp. 677-89. Publishes the expanded version as it appears in MS. 82-2-5 of the Biblioteca Colombina.

WALBERG, EMMANUEL. "Juan de la Cueva et son *Ejemplar poético*," *Lunds Universitets Arsskrift*, XXXIX (1904), 1-113. The basic critical text and study of the *Poet's Guide*.

WARDROPPER, BRUCE W. "Juan de la Cueva y el drama histórico," *Nueva Revista de Filología Hispánica*, IX (1955), 149-56. An excellent article in which the ideological tension of the *Comedia del reto de Zamora* is investigated.

WATSON, ANTHONY IRVINE. *Juan de la Cueva and the Portuguese Succession* (London: Tamesis, 1971). The literary and political parallels in this important and excellently documented study are convincingly argued. This is a revision of the author's doctoral dissertation, "Political Implications of the Drama of Juan de la Cueva." University of London (London, 1956).

WILLIAMS, ROBERT H. "Francisco de Cáceres, Niccolò Franco and Juan de la Cueva," *Hispanic Review*, XXVII (1959), 194-99. A valuable contribution which discusses Cueva's models for *Sannio's Journey*.

WULFF, FREDRIK A. "De las rimas de Juan de la Cueva, Primera Parte," *Homenaje a Menéndez y Pelayo*, II (Madrid: Suárez, 1899), 143-48. An important article in which the author speculates that Cueva's volume of poetry may never have been circulated.

————. "Poèmes inédits de Juan de la Cueva," *Lunds Universitets Arsskrift*, XXIII (1887), i-c, 1-64. Contains the basic biographical data and description of the Cueva MSS of the Biblioteca Colombina. Excerpts from the complete *Viaje de Sannio* are included. Texts based on MS. 82-2-5 are printed for the first time.

2. Studies Which Touch on Juan de la Cueva:

CASTRO, AMÉRICO. "Algunas observaciones acerca del concepto del honor en los siglos XVI y XVII," *Revista de Filología Española,* III (1916), 18-19. Concerns the *Comedy of the Defamer.*

CHAYTOR, H. J. *Dramatic Theory in Spain* (Cambridge: Cambridge University Press, 1925). Contains excerpts from the *Poets' Guide.*

COSSÍO, JOSÉ MARÍA DE. *Fábulas mitológicas en España* (Madrid: Espasa-Calpe, 1952). A rather superficial coverage of some of the myths treated by Cueva. The ballads are practically ignored.

COSTER, ADOLPHE. *Fernando de Herrera (el Divino) 1534-1597* (Paris: Champion, 1908). A very valuable, scholarly study which examines the literary, social, and political world of which Cueva was a part.

CRAWFORD, J. P. WICKERSHAM. *Spanish Drama before Lope de Vega,* 2nd ed., rev. (Philadelphia: University of Pennsylvania Press, 1967). Warren T. McCready's Bibliographical Supplement is a valuable addition to this uncritical survey which devotes only seven pages to Cueva.

FUCILLA, JOSEPH G. *Estudios sobre el petrarquismo en España* (Madrid: *Revista de Filología Española* [Anejo LXXII], 1960). Establishes that Cueva utilized all the Petrarchan conventions.

GALLARDO Y BLANCO, BARTOLOMÉ JOSÉ. *Ensayo de una biblioteca española de libros raros y curiosos.* 4 vols. (Madrid: Rivadeneyra, 1863-1869), II (1866), cols. 637-736. The basic and indispensable bibliography of Cueva's texts, although it is not definitive.

HERMENEGILDO, ALFREDO. *Los trágicos españoles del siglo XVI* (Madrid: Raycar, 1961). An uneven survey of tragedians of the sixteenth century.

ICAZA, FRANCISCO A. DE. "Gutierre de Cetina y Juan de la Cueva," *Boletín de la Real Academia Española,* III (1916), 315-35. See next entry.

————. *Sucesos reales que parecen imaginados, de Gutierre de Cetina, Juan de la Cueva y Mateo Alemán* (Madrid: Fortanet, 1919). A convenient summary of all the biographical data Icaza gathered on Cueva.

MEDÈL DEL CASTILLO, FRANCISCO. *Índice general alfabético de todos los títulos de comedias,* ed. John M. Hill. In *Revue Hispanique,* LXXV (1929), 144-369. Cueva's play *The Death of Ajax Telamon* is attributed to Antonio de la Cueva.

MENÉNDEZ PELAYO, MARCELINO. *Historia de la poesía hispanoamericana*, 2 vols. (Madrid: Librería General de Victoriano Suárez, 1911). Reprints (I, 33-35) a portion of Cueva's fifth epistle.

MENÉNDEZ PIDAL, RAMÓN. *La leyenda de los Infantes de Lara*, 2nd ed. (Madrid: Hernando, 1934), pp. 121-26. A valuable discussion of Cueva's play.

MITTERER, RICHARD. *Die Sage von Bernardo del Carpio im spanischen Drama des XVI und XVII Jahrhunderts* (Würzburg: G. Grasser, 1930), pp. 193-97. A general survey of the Bernardo del Carpio legend in the Spanish drama of the Golden Age. Sparse treatment of Cueva's play.

MONTIANO Y LUYANDO, AGUSTÍN. *Discursos sobre las tragedias españolas* (Madrid: Joseph de Orga, 1750), pp. 16-23. Cueva's tragedies are discussed superficially.

MORLEY, S. GRISWOLD. "Strophes in the Spanish Drama before Lope de Vega," *Homenaje ofrecido a Menéndez Pidal*. 3 vols. (Madrid: Hernando, 1925), I, 505-31. An important discussion of Cueva's strophic preferences is included.

PÉREZ DE AYALA, RAMÓN. *Las máscaras*. 2 vols. (Madrid: Renacimiento, 1924), II, 91-97. Cueva's rôle in the evolution of the Spanish drama is considered.

PIERCE, FRANCIS WILLIAM. *La poesía épica del siglo de oro*, 2nd ed., rev. (Madrid: Gredos, 1968). Includes an excellent bibliography of critical opinion on Cueva's *Conquest of Andalusia*.

REIG, CAROLA. *El cantar de Sancho II y cerco de Zamora* (Madrid: Revista de Filología Española [Anejo XXXVII], 1947). Contains a plot summary of Cueva's play and discusses the epic sources.

RODRÍGUEZ MARÍN, FRANCISCO. *Luis Barahona de Soto. Estudio biográfico, bibliográfico y crítico* (Madrid: Sucesores de Rivadeneyra, 1903). An important list (pp. 242-49) of the poems by Cueva attributed erroneously to Barahona de Soto in MS. 33-180-6 of the Biblioteca del Palacio Arzobispal in Seville is included.

————. *Nuevos datos para las biografías de cien autores* (Madrid: Tipografía de la Revista de Archivos, Bibliotecas y Museos, 1923), pp. 513-16. Reproduces Cueva's petition to the City of Seville to subsidize the cost of printing his *Conquest of Andalusia*.

SÁNCHEZ ESCRIBANO, FEDERICO and ALBERTO PORQUERAS MAYO. *Preceptiva dramática española del renacimiento y el baroco* (Madrid: Gredos, 1967), pp. 115-22. Reprints a fragment of the *Poets' Guide*.

SHERGOLD, N. D. *A History of the Spanish Stage from Medieval Times until the End of the Seventeenth Century* (Oxford:

Clarendon, 1967). The basic reference which takes into account all that has been learned about the Peninsular stage.

3. Useful Background Materials:

CANTER, HOWARD VERNON. *Rhetorical Elements in the Tragedies of Seneca.* University of Illinois Studies in Language and Literature, No. 10 (Urbana: University of Illinois Press, 1925). An excellent résumé of Cueva's most important model.

DEFERRARI, HARRY AUSTIN. *The Sentimental Moor in Spanish Literature before 1600* (Philadelphia: University of Pennsylvania Press, 1927). An interesting examination of the new attitude of tolerance of the Moor in Spanish literature of this period.

GREEN, OTIS H. *Spain and the Western Tradition.* 4 vols. (Madison: University of Wisconsin Press, 1968). Indispensable for an understanding of Cueva's cultural heritage.

HIGHET, GILBERT. *The Classical Tradition, Greek and Roman Influences on Western Literature* (New York: Oxford University Press, 1949). Essential for an understanding of the manner in which Greek and Latin influences molded literary tastes during Cueva's age.

PFANDL, LUDWIG. *Historia de la literatura nacional española en la edad de oro,* tr. Jorge Rubió Balaguer (Barcelona: Sucesores de Juan Gili, 1933). A useful general history of literature of the Spanish Golden Age.

SÁNCHEZ, JOSÉ. *Academias literarias del siglo de oro español* (Madrid: Gredos, 1961). Provides excellent insights into the significance of literary academies for writers such as Cueva.

Index

Items appearing only in the Bibliography are excluded.

175

Index   177